"I am delighted to pen a review of this book which I found to be beautifully written and from the heart.

Paula's connection with these sentient beings is captivating and if you have ever wanted to hug a tree please read this book first as we do need to ask if it's OK with them and listen.

I also liked Paula's personal narrative of her own spiritual journey which added to the enjoyment"

Colleen Guy

Shamanic Practitioner, Transformational Coach & Trainer

"I love this beautiful book. I want to give a copy to everyone I know! Very readable, it's the sort to keep by the bedside and dip into constantly, like a box of delicious chocolates.

The ancient yews have urgent messages for the whole of humanity: each yew, in its own wise way, speaks of peace, harmony, loving kindness and the interconnectedness of all Life.

While these uplifting messages are particularly apposite in this time of crisis, and for meditation, they also provide a beautiful heart-centred focus as we go about our everyday lives.

In this time of crisis we are rediscovering the joy and peace of taking time in Nature and remembering that we are part of it. Paula's experience shows that love and wisdom surround us and is constantly available to us if we simply trust and take the time to open and listen to the trees and plants.

I heartily recommend this wonderful book."

Marion Eaton

Award Winning Author

"This is a book that will talk to your souls!

Paula Flint very cleverly writes with such an elegant, yet approachable style that will convert any sceptical souls around. If I started reading this book with an open mind, I can certainly say that by the final chapter, something quite special had happened in terms of my perception of the symbiose between the yew trees, all living creatures and us, mankind.

This is a book written as a personal narrative which takes you gently into Flint's world and spiritual journey sharing her incredible gifts and notably her faculty to communicate and share the very important messages from the everlasting yew trees she has connected with. Flint, not only uses her sense of humour, and totally understands that some souls might see her as "a bonkers tree hugger", but it is without any extravagance that she reveals the messages she has been tasked to share.

This is the writing of a very courageous and tenacious woman whose incredible life journey is depicted into a relaxing, peaceful yet intriguing book to read. Flint enables you to discover and understand the world of those mythical trees within history whilst giving us snapshots of her life, her inner spirituality, her wisdom within her psychic abilities.

She totally personalises the yew trees with each of her mesmerising photos, their tree names and the attributes she gives to them. The poignant messages they convey will make you wonder and look at the world around you with hopeful eyes and souls."

KLS Fuerte
Author of: Never Saw You Coming, Now Live With That!

———————————————————

WHAT IF
TREES
HAVE SOULS?

CONVERSATIONS WITH
ANCIENT YEWS AND THEIR
PROFOUND WORDS OF WISDOM

Paula Flint

HIDDEN
VOICES

"...It is ESSENTIAL that the world hear this plea for the good of all.   It is of great importance that mankind hear our words, but of greater importance that they act on them..."

"...I may be the last on your "List of Yews to Visit", but my message is without doubt the most urgent of all the messages you have so far received.   We prevail, implore and beseech you to communicate our truths..."

Ankerwycke Yew, Runnymede

MY MISSION

… is to keep my word in spreading the important messages from the Ancient, Notable and Veteran yew trees across the planet.

And...

do my bit to support in the planting of trees across areas suffering deforestation, in particular, endangered Orangutans.

Contents

What If Trees Have Souls? 12

My Journey 16

Yew Classifications 17

Chalice Well 18

Compton Dundon 20

Crowhurst E Sussex Ancient 24

Crowhurst E Sussex Veteran [1] 28

Crowhurst E Sussex Veteran [2] 30

Wilmington 34

Herstmonceux 37

1993 39

Northiam 40

Lamberhurst 43

1997 45

Capel 46

Etchingham 48

1998 51

Petham 52

Elmsted Ancient 1 54

2001 57

Elmsted Ancient 2 58

Elmsted Veteran 1 60

Elmsted Veteran 2 62

January 2002 65

Buxted 66

Chailey Ancient 68

Chailey Veteran 70

March 2002 73

Rotherfield 74

Crowhurst Surrey 76

2003 79

Tandridge Ancient 80

Contents...

Tandridge Veteran 82

2004 85

Kennington Ancient 86

Kennington Veteran 1 88

2005 91

Kennington Veteran 2 92

Kennington Veteran 3 94

2006 97

Molash Ancient 1 98

Molash Ancient 2 100

Molash Ancient 3 102

Molash Ancient 4 103

2007 105

Molash Ancient 5 106

Molash Ancient 6 108

2010 111

Ulcombe Ancient 1 112

Ulcombe Ancient 2 114

2011 117

Ulcombe Veteran 118

Ulcombe Notable 120

November 2012 121

Harrietsham Ancient 122

Harrietsham Veteran 124

October 2013 126

Broomfield 128

Leeds 130

November 2013 133

Loose 136

Wivelsfield Ancient 138

Wivelsfield Veteran 142

Wivelsfield Notable 144

May 2017 147

Ardingly 148

Contents...

Ankerwycke 151

How I Communicate 157

Thoughts & Musings 162

Fact & Fiction 164

Talking To Trees Project 165

About the Author 166

One Last Thing 168

Acknowledgements 169

WHAT IF TREES HAVE SOULS?

Be prepared to be transported into the inner sanctum of trees.

A world where trees are able to converse with one another... and with humans.

I can talk to trees...

Telepathically...

In fact, so can you, should you choose to expand your awareness and focus.

I've been talking with tree spirits for several years and what originally started out as an interesting hobby took on a darker tone after a dialogue with the Ancient yew at Ankerwycke.

The Ancients have important messages they wish mankind to hear and hopefully act upon.

To this end, they decided I should facilitate their words of wisdom. and become their 'ambassador'. Not a task I particularly relished and the thought of putting myself out for ridicule by those less 'spiritual' wasn't something that particularly appealed. It still doesn't to be honest. As the saying goes: "I'd rather be behind the camera than in front of it". However, I promised to relay their communications, so here we are...

Some of the yews I've conversed with are several thousand years old and have many insights and observations. Their messages of love, peace and blessings are tinged with tidings of portent should we not change our ways.

With a vast array of knowledge accumulated through the passage of time, they have their own language, individual names and a sense of purpose on this earth plane. These sentient beings are non-judgemental, display individual personalities and have a sense of humour.

I consider myself blessed with being able to pass on the thoughts, observations and profound words of wisdom from some of the oldest trees on our planet and invite you to explore what the Ancient yews believe we should be doing to evolve, co-create and co-exist... not only to increase our chances of survival but those of the myriad of other species we reside with.

It is said we are all connected and as One.

My work is thus done.

However, our work together is just beginning...

For as long as I can remember I've always had a thing about trees. Have absolutely no idea why but I feel completely at peace when wandering through the woods and outside in nature, so I suppose this experience should come as no great surprise.

It's early evening on the last day of a holiday and I'm standing on the fringes of a beach in the Indian Ocean watching the evening sky. The sun is slowly dipping below the horizon and the clouds are streaked with orange, pink and various shades of blue.

Next to me is a magnificent banyan tree, it's long tendrils touching the ground swirling around like eddies in a rock pool.

Admiring its form, I step forward to touch it and place both hands on its trunk to mentally say goodbye and express my admiration in how it's able to regenerate.

In the calm silence that follows and over the gentle lapping of the soft waves breaking on the sand, words form in my head.

By now I'm used to hearing and receiving messages from spirit, but... from a tree?

My Journey

Originally, I had the intention to only include conversations with the Ancient yews. However, the Veteran and Notable yews also had relevant messages to impart, so it feels fitting to include their messages as well. In addition, instead of listing the yews alphabetically I've decided to include them chronologically as I feel this helps to show how the dialogues and communication developed over the course of time.

For those of you who may be wondering; no, I didn't just wake up one bright sunny morning to discover that, out of the blue, I could telepathically talk to trees. Had that happened I think I would have been well spooked! So, I've included snippets about my spiritual journey over the last 20 or so years to show a glimpse into the path I've followed resulting in this amazing gift and culminating in this compilation of messages.

That said, I do believe the energies on the planet are speeding up, and by that I mean we're all becoming ever more intuitive and able to sense things more easily. People are also more willing to explore areas previously classed as 'hippy dippy' such as meditation, mindfulness and the Law of Attraction. The spiritual community is growing exponentially year on year, aided by eminent figures such as Eckhart Tolle and Wayne Dyer, all helping to bridge the scientific and spiritual gap.

Therefore, it would actually come as no surprise to learn of those who may wake up one morning to suddenly find they can communicate with trees and/or other beings of nature. Indeed, I encourage everyone to have a go and try to connect, on some level, with tree energy.

Yew Classifications

A yew is notoriously difficult to age, the primary classification being its girth, although this is not set in stone as it can differ according to growing conditions and a yew's ability to become dormant for long periods of time (see Crowhurst Surrey yew p.76).

One such example is an Ancient in Norbury Park, South London which became partially uprooted in 1720 and then sprouted a new branch in 2018, some 300 years later.

Deemed by many to be one of the oldest living things in Britain, yews can live to over five thousand years old. The 'Ancient Yew Group (AYG)' have classified yews into three groups; Ancient, Veteran and Notable based on age, girth and significance.

However, due to the nature of how yews deteriorate and regenerate this can be a tricky enterprise. When a yew fragments and different sections can be seen, the hollow trunk denotes a particular stage of growth, slow-growing and typically extremely old.

This also complicates deciding where and how to measure the girth, therefore an age overlap exists between delineating Ancient/Veteran and Veteran/Notable. Yews in various stages of growth are evidenced throughout the book.

Ancient: 800+ years old, girth 7m+

Veteran: 500 – 1200 years, girth 4.9m+

Notable: 300 – 700 years, girth 3.1m – 3.

CHALICE WELL

SOMERSET

"Be True..."

Yesterday was spent visiting Stonehenge. The first day of a planned weekend in the West Country which has left me feeling 'out of sorts' with the world. Not only was it a day packed with drama, but the energy of the stones felt sad and depressing. It's only when looking back at the photos I realise how much time I spent standing *outside* the circle.

Nothing like the Easter weekend I remember from my early twenties when four of us arrived on a misty, cold dawn morn and sat on a stone watching the sun come up. No-one around, eerily quiet and spell binding. Now it's regimented, with

eagle eyed 'stone bouncers' intimidatingly strutting their stuff.

So far, today has seen Glastonbury ticked off the to-do-list. Next up is Glastonbury Tor and Chalice Well. The Well is at the foot of the Tor so I've decided to start there before summoning my strength to walk up the steep hill. I know nothing about Chalice Well apart from everyone saying how wonderful it is, so I'm pleasantly surprised to find a peaceful set of garden 'rooms' with an actual well that's reputed to be around 2,000 years old.

It's a warm, sunny day in May and I'm wandering aimlessly back down the garden on my way out, when I come across two rather magnificent yew trees standing like sentinels either side of a pathway near the entrance. Before I know it, I'm walking towards the yew to the right of the path, palms open and 'tuning in' to its energy.

YEW MESSAGE:

Gender: Male
Year: c. AD 1,418
Name: N/A

"Wise is the master who walks the path of dreams... and once there, sips from the cup that overfloweth with healing for mind body and soul. Rest easy and spend time frolicking with frivolous thoughts that are not wasted, but are vital nourishment for the soul. Every step is a path walked on old souls. Be true to yourself, be true to nature and be kind to the earth for remember, it is your nourishment."

Conversation over, I chat to a volunteer at the ticket booth to see if she has any information on the yews, and inadvertently let slip they were Father and Son (I've talked to the Father). The rather astonished volunteer confirms this to be the case. It seems the Father has been measured to be at least 600 years old* and both yews stand guard as a portal to the Well itself.

strictly speaking, 600 years old isn't classed as 'Ancient' but it seems appropriate to include him as this marks the first of my yew encounters.

COMPTON DUNDON

ST. ANDREWS PARISH CHURCH, SOMERSET

"Follow Your Wishes & Dreams"

I've climbed the Tor; hot, steep and windy at the top but I'm glad I did as the stunning views were well worth the effort. However, instead of finishing for the day, I now find myself on my way to a small village called Compton Dundon. Not something I'd had on my list of "Places to Visit" until speaking to the volunteer on the gate at Chalice Well. *"If you're interested in yew trees, you might want to visit the Ancient yew at Compton Dundon"* she said... *"It's not far from here, maybe 15-20 minutes"*. I can't say I've been interested in yew trees *specifically*, but nothing else is planned and besides, I'm intrigued.

I'm struggling to find the yew and beginning to feel a tad perplexed. I've diligently followed the sat-nav to the village and I'm sure I must be getting close as I've seen the house name 'Yew Cottage'. Having said that, my sat-nav *does* have a mind of its own and I have absolutely zero faith in its ability to get me to where I want to go in the quickest route or without trying to send me down a canal.

However, there are no signs pointing to a church or an ancient yew and I'm now out of the other side of the village. One side road looks promising but no joy, so I turn the car around for the second time. This is becoming a bit of a mission and I'm half tempted to give up when a gut feeling tells me to take a different side turning. I drive past the village hall, along a mile or so of fields, round a tight corner and, by sheer luck, I catch sight of the church with an enormous yew looming in front of it.

It being such a pleasant day and in no rush, I spend some time just sitting underneath the canopy enjoying the moment before leaning against it and tuning in. I sense a strong, powerful, deep energy with overtones of an all-knowing wisdom. In fact, I've been here so long I've had two separate dialogues and been so absorbed and engrossed it's only as I'm leaving I notice the sign at the base marked 'Ancient Yew'.

However, before leaving and on the spur of the moment I try the church door and discover to my surprise and delight it's unlocked. I creep inside and spy a framed document nailed to the wall stating the yew to be 1,700 years old. Wonderfully ancient!

YEW MESSAGE:

Gender: Male
Year: AD 317
Name: N/A

"Wishes and hopes all come true for those who serve God's highest purpose. It is with sadness and regret that life struggles for those who do not follow the highest paths. Be sure to follow your wishes and dreams to attain peace and happiness. Life has crosses to bear, just as Jesus had his cross to bear. We must remember that life struggles are but a blip in the history of time. We are all connected. We are One. We are Eternal."

ADDITIONAL DIALOGUE:

"Rivers of ice..

Valleys of water...

Mountains of ash...

Trees are Immortal...

We transcend time and space.

THE ANCIENT ONES MUST BE HEARD."

The end of summer is slowly creeping in and I'm sitting quietly meditating.

It's mid-afternoon and, although sunny, there's a chilly breeze so I've positioned a reclining chair in a patch of sun streaming through the open patio door and am lounging sleepily, feet up on a footstool.

From out of nowhere, I hear the distinct message:

"you need to seek out Ancient yew trees as they have important messages they want to share with the world".

I'm starting to wonder if I had nodded off and been dreaming when the final words from the Compton Dundon yew loudly interrupt my thoughts ...

*"The Ancient Ones **must** be heard".*

CROWHURST

ST. GEORGE'S CHURCH, EAST SUSSEX

"Gratitude"

Living only a few miles away, I'm still unsure why it's taken me over twenty years before coming to visit this amazing Ancient.

I like to touch a tree when communicating as I receive a stronger energy connection, however this tree is railed and I'm prevented from getting to the trunk.   Thankfully, it has large sprawling limbs embracing the floor which I can reach and this is sufficient for me to connect to her energy.

Local history states the yew to be between 1,200 and 1,500 years old with the first church on this site being 771.   This perfectly ties in with how old the yew believes itself to be.

YEW MESSAGE:

Gender: Female
Year: AD 739
Name: "Surgeon"

"Revere all life for it is a gift and an honour to be here. You take and take and take. Do not take for granted. You must appreciate more and learn gratitude. Gratitude is your meaning and your purpose. All are linked. Linked as inexorably as the stars and the moon. Be with meaning, go with gratitude, live with purpose."

ADDITIONAL DIALOGUE:

"Yes... that is my message. It has been good to talk to you."

(Feeling brave, I ask a few questions) :

Me: [You have been here a long time, you must have seen a lot of good and bad?]

"I have been here a long time and seen good and not so good. There is never bad, only not so good."

Me: [How old are you?]

"I believe I have been here since AD 739"

Me: [Va con Dios]

"Thank you... I am always with God. Go with Grace Little One."

(Note: this is the first time I am referred to as 'Little One')

Since my first dialogue, I have enrolled in weekly watercolour painting classes and, synchronicity being what it is, they are held in the church hall. Depending on the weather and other commitments, I sometimes stop for additional chats. On one such occasion it occurs to me to ask what her name is (which led me to ask others in subsequent conversations):

"I am glad to see you are up and walking about again [I recently underwent knee surgery]... *my name is 'Surgeon'"*

Me: [Surgeon?]

"Yes, that's correct, 'Surgeon' - I slice through the ravages of time and fix what I can with whatever energies I can bring to bear on the issue for the greatest good of all."

Me: [It looks as though someone has cut you open with a knife!]

"Ha-ha, yes, I certainly live up to my name!"

Me: [Do you feel the cold?]

"We do not feel it, nor do we fear it. We have foresight to a certain extent. These coming months will be bitter and colder than you have felt for some time, however you will get through it as thousands before you have done. Stay sheltered and fear not. Be aware the wildlife may need protection too".

HISTORY

Croghyrst, Croherste, Crohest or Crowhurste as the village was originally known, lies on a country road between Hastings and Battle and until 1066 the manor was owned by King Harold.   Prior to the Battle of Hastings, the Normans completely destroyed the manor and Hope Muntz reports in "The Golden Warrior" that the Reeve was hanged from "the great yew tree" for refusing to tell where the treasure was hidden. In 1412 Henry IV gave the land to Sir John Pelham who built the current church, and a picturesque insight into Crowhurst church life in the 19th century is given by Madge. E. Newman, B.A, a former head mistress of the village school:

"And the village church, low towered and small
Stands close to a ruined mansion wall,
On a grassy bank, in a peaceful nook
Just above a rush-fringed brook.
Half hid by the very largest yew
I ever saw in my life - or you.

And the old clerk wears a surtout grey
And the white old men in the gallery pray,
And sing out of tune just a verse or two
Of the old version always, and not the new
And this is a picture of Crowhurst true."

CROWHURST
[VETERAN 1]
ST. GEORGE'S CHURCH, EAST SUSSEX

"Practise Loving Kindness"

It didn't occur to me at the time of conversing with this lady to make a full note of our conversation back and forth regarding her age, however there is definitely some confusion... She's uncertain whether the year she was birthed was AD 349 or AD 648.

She has finally decided it is AD 349, however this would make her an Ancient rather than a Veteran.   Who am I to argue?

YEW MESSAGE:

Gender: Female
Year: AD 349
Name: "Heliotrope"

"Be at peace with the world.   You are but children playing in the sands of time.   Your hopes and dreams are like will-o'-the-wisps... fragile and easily vanquished.

Be at peace... practise loving kindness – to yourself and all others."

CROWHURST
[VETERAN 2]
ST. GEORGE'S CHURCH, EAST SUSSEX

"Love Is All There Is"

Like her sister, this yew is also having issues with deciding how old she is. She's reported to be around 600 years old but thinks she's between 350 – 500. However, I'm having the overwhelming feeling that she's 720.

YEW MESSAGE:

Gender: Female
Year: AD 1297 (?)
Name: "Windswept"

"Love is like the waves on an ocean. They come, they go. Each wave is there in it's moment and then is lost. And then another comes. You may not feel like you are loving all the time, but like the ocean beneath

the waves, love is all there is.   It is there within you whether you are aware or not.

The more waves you can surf, the more at peace you will be and, yes, happiness comes with being at peace."

"BE TRUE"

"FOLLOW YOUR WISHES AND DREAMS"

"GRATITUDE"

"PRACTISE LOVING KINDNESS"

"LOVE IS ALL THERE IS"

Following my epiphany to speak to the yews, the laptop is out and I'm busily researching where I can find these Ancient trees. I can feel a sense of excitement and a purpose.

The first yew to appear in the search is Ankerwycke, up by the river Thames. It sounds impressive; quite old and steeped in history, but... it's quite a drive away. I keep looking.

Well, would you believe it – there's a website dedicated to Ancient yew trees! Amazingly it has a registered list of all the Ancient, Veteran and Notable yews across the country. What a find!

The yews are listed by county, so I'm now studying a map of the local counties and making a list.

There seem to be quite a few so that should keep me nicely occupied for a while, with a bonus of exploring the local countryside!

WILMINGTON

ST. MARY & ST PETER'S CHURCH, EAST SUSSEX

"Peace & Harmony"

I'm now armed with a list of "Yews to Visit" but that's about it. With no real plan I've decided the best course of action is to just start working my way out from home.

So after starting at Crowhurst, Wilmington is the next port of call as I'm familiar with the village (and it's a good excuse to be able to pop into the little crystal shop nearby!). However, I don't recall ever seeing any sign mentioning an ancient yew. Or the church for that matter. Hmm.

I've finally worked out where to go but it's such a narrow lane I've squeezed the car as tight as I can against a wall, wing mirrors in. After a muddy climb up a dubious steep path I find what must be the back gate to the churchyard. It's not difficult to spot the yew; large, sprawling and pretty much the only tree in the churchyard. A couple of branches are held up with long poles and it looks a bit bedraggled. I wander round, taking a few photos then find a comfy limb and settle in for a chat. I sense this yew is male but he has an odd feminine energy to it. He feels lovely, light-hearted and enthusiastic.

YEW MESSAGE:

Gender: Male
Year: AD 393
Name: N/A

"You are welcome to sit with me a while. It has been a while since anyone has requested my knowledge. Yes, I am a grandfather... many times greater than you can imagine. I have seen a lot of things come to pass. I have been here since the three hundreds. The exact year I forget.

I would like the world to hear that peace and harmony reign supreme. I would like the world to hear that loving kindness is a bitter sweet pill to swallow, but it is necessary for the world, humanity, to evolve. They need to evolve into softer, kinder, more generous of spirit beings. Humans need each other for support. As do trees.

There is an underlying essence of "All That Is" between all energy and it is our duty to preserve and nurture this essence. For it is this essence that sustains us in all that we do and all that we are. This may be too esoteric for many to understand, but that is my message. It is my message of hope...

I'm glad you liked it and approve.

Me: [Do trees have 'tree' names?]

Yes, trees have names, but they would be incomprehensible to humans. Your auditory capabilities are not in tune and you would not be able to decipher or understand the noise of our song. It would sound like a mere rumble of noise. A bit like your Welsh perhaps! Our language is old. Literally as old as the hills. And beyond.

(He was quite right – when he told me his name it sounded like "oulaglougghheeahhh").

It has been nice talking to you.   I have appreciated your company."

Me: [Thank you Ancient One.   One last question - do you get lonely?]

"Loneliness and being alone are not the same.   I am alone yes, but not lonely.   How can I be lonely when I am connected to All That Is.

We are timeless.   We are eternal."

I've finished writing down his message and feel compelled to send him some Reiki as a thank you for connecting with me.

As I sense the Reiki flowing into him I feel a strange pulsing sensation in my arms. The best I can describe the feeling is as though there's an additional liquid flowing through my veins, alongside another heartbeat. I'm totally unaware of how long I sat, connected, sharing our energy until I realise I've got cramp and have to end the session.

Conversation over, I wander inside the church, founded in c.AD 1000, almost a thousand years ago to serve the Saxon settlement of 'Winetone', the original name of Wilmington as recorded in the Doomsday Book. Also there is a framed document dated July 1993 stating the yew to be 1600 years old with a girth of more than 23' at it's base. Pretty much ties in with the age this yew has determined.

HERSTMONCEUX

ALL SAINT'S PARISH CHURCH, EAST SUSSEX

"Develop Awareness In All That You Do"

It's now the beginning of November and, naively, I had assumed (from talking to deciduous trees previously) that being evergreen yews are awake all year round and deciduous trees go to sleep or hibernate. Not quite so!

This Ancient-Grandfather energy is definitely in a deep slumber, well below the surface and I feel quite guilty at waking him.

Thankfully, he isn't at all fussed about being roused, although a bit croaky from not having talked for a while!

YEW MESSAGE:

Gender: Male
Year: AD 217(?)
Name: N/A

"I have not spoken to anyone in a very long time... 500, 600 hundred years perhaps. It is good to break one's pattern. Nature has a way of taking you off on a blissful slumber. Years pass into centuries without one noticing.

We are but a seed in the spectrum of time. A pinprick in the maelstrom of all that is passing by. A light beam on the path of enlightenment.

It is our job, no, our role, to play out the wonders of The Universe in the passage of All That Is. Over and over. We should be adhering to and learning the lessons and gifts of learning what knowledge brings to the world.

You humans have much to learn and yet the learning is there, but you do not feel it. You do not accept it. You do not absorb it. You play out to your imaginations without considering the consequences.

You must be more aware. Develop awareness in all that you do. Do that and your learning pattern will start on the path to greatness."

1993

When was your dark night of the soul?

Mine was October 1993. After ten years of struggling, a major hiccup with my business has left me homeless, car-less, job-less and teetering on the edge of bankruptcy. Hardly surprising, I feel hugely stressed and needless to say, my health has suffered as a consequence. Lots of minor symptoms, nothing major, but debilitating none the less.

Pottering about in a bookshop today I've discovered a book which seems spot on and lists most of the ailments I'm suffering from (Candida Albicans which can be stress induced). From what I've read it seems a strict food elimination diet may be of benefit, however it's quite a daunting prospect. No sugar, gluten or dairy. Grim!!!

Albeit tough, the diet does actually seem to be working. However I'm feeling fairly miserable and sorry for myself so have decided to visit a local sauna as a pick-me-up treat.

While frazzling on the lower bench I've overheard a conversation between two ladies above me. It seems there's a local practitioner who has started doing Kinesiology and is looking for clients to practise on.

Kinesiology?? Never heard of it. However, when needs must I'll consider anything, however weird it sounds!

NORTHIAM

ST MARY'S CHURCH, EAST SUSSEX

"Generosity of Spirit"

It's a week later... another grey November day and a subtle smell of bonfire night is still hanging in the air.

I've been surprised how few Ancient female yew trees there are. This Ancient has a very soft, definitely feminine energy but there's also an aloofness about her which is unnerving. Similar to a Goddess and unlike anything I've previously encountered. We're also having a bit of an issue working out her age, but she's finally settled on AD 798.

I always make a point of going inside each church in the hunt for information. The Wilmington and Compton Dundon yews had certificates showing their age (to the best of their knowledge). However, this isn't something you can always rely on so, by trial and error, I've devised a method of working out how old they are.

I started off asking the yews their age directly, however most have such a vague sense of time I had to abandon that plan fairly early on.   Other time line methods also proved fruitless.   In the end I was guided to try 'balancing' on it.   By placing one hand on my heart centre and keeping the other on the tree, I ask a series of questions and, depending on whether I sway forwards or backwards, I'm able to pinpoint the century and year.   It's a bit time consuming and rudimentary but seems to work (see Crowhurst, Surrey Ancient p.76).

YEW MESSAGE:

Gender: Female
Year: AD 798
Name: N/A

"It is an odd request [to communicate with me] *but one I am happy to oblige with.*

My message for the Universe, for that is where we all reside, is one of generosity and kindness of spirit.

You are here today because we are connected.   We are connected as one being, we are ethereal, we are joined. We are singing the same song, little did you know it.   We are paving the way for future generations to evolve into kinder beings.

We, the Ancient Ones, are wisdom personified.

We testify to all that has gone on before and we will testify to all that follows you.

The age will come when man hath no choice but to bend his knee and submit to peace and loving kindness.   Bear my words; that if man fails in this then he will fail in himself.   For it is written in The Universe that this Must come to pass if man is to survive.

Peace is fragile, like the trill of a songbird.

Kindness is as elusive as a summer flower hidden in snow.

41

I wish Peace and Loving Kindness to all mankind.

[Offering Reiki]...

"Yes, it is fitting that we exchange energies."

I'm giving my usual Reiki blessing when, out of the blue, I'm being transported into what can only be described as 'tree form'. It feels as though the skeletal veins on a leaf are spreading along my arms and through the rest of my body.

I leave with the sensation of being extremely tall with an unprecedented 360 degree awareness. Fascinating.

LAMBERHURST

ST MARY'S CHURCH, EAST SUSSEX

"Practise Loving Kindness"

I have had the most unexpected afternoon. Not only has it been a beautiful sunny day visiting this jovial yew, but I've been privileged to have enjoyed a private piano performance in a stunning church location.

Whilst chatting to this playful ancient I could hear the strains of a piano delicately interrupting my thoughts. Venturing into the church I discovered there was a concert taking place later that evening and the pianist was busy practising scales and bits of what I suppose he was going to play that evening, although I confess it was nothing I actually recognised. The local vicar was arranging seating and, seeing me standing there gawping, kindly drew up a chair for me to sit and listen!

YEW MESSAGE:

Gender: Male
Year: AD 1119
Name: N/A

"I'm well Little One"

Me: [Why Little One?]

"You are little in stature and also little in wisdom and years.   Ha ha! We all know you as 'Little One'.   Oh yes, we are all connected through Mother Earth... we can read all things of nature and spirit.

Your cause is great.   Many of you are struggling to achieve enlightenment.   But what is this elusive thing you seek?   Is it not better to seek to improve your generosity of nature?   Your willingness to help others in need?   Your support for those less well off than yourself?

Why do you seek something so intangible when the path to true greatness lies in helping others.   You should be practising loving kindness to all others irrespective of race, class and upbringing.   This is the path to enlightenment.   When you bring light to all those around you, then have you truly fulfilled your destiny."

1997

It's a year since the birth of my daughter and through a chance conversation with a fellow mum I'm beginning to suspect I may have post natal depression.

A tearful trip to the Doctor confirms my suspicions and following a course of tablets the depression has now lifted. However, I'm starting to feel the pressures of working full-time and caring for a toddler.

Not wanting to take further medication I'm investigating other alternative therapies. I'm no longer strictly following the elimination diet but still having kinesiology (with a side helping of reflexology) as it's quite effective in calming some remaining digestive ailments. My T'ai Chi instructor is also an acupuncturist and regular sessions are resolving hormonal issues. Not bad for someone who isn't fond of feet and can't abide needles! However, that still leaves the emotional side of things.

My kinesiologist has started giving me Reiki. Not something I've previously come across and pretty much unheard of in most circles but, interestingly, I'm finding it's helping me to keep calm under duress and overall much less stressed.

CAPEL

CHURCH OF ST. THOMAS A BECKETT, KENT

"Follow Your Heart"

This delightful church has *definitely* taken some finding, but is extremely charming and worth a visit if you happen to be in the vicinity.

Sir Thomas Beckett is said to have preached beneath this tree, however I hope it was substantially warmer than today's cold mid- November day!

Although a fairly ancient yew with a large hollow interior, he sounds surprisingly youthful and I've been touched he's acknowledged how freezing cold it is . My breath is hanging, making misty trails in the air as I walk and I give grateful thanks for finger-less gloves!!

YEW MESSAGE:

Gender: Male
Year: AD 229
Name: N/A

"Hello Little One... yes, I have heard of your coming.   Blessed be that you have come here on this blustery cold day.   Your coming is foretold on the winds and in the seeds of the earth.   It is a good deed to bring our words to the world of man.

I prophesize that man will survive and flourish if he follows his heart and not listen to greed or follow the path of acquiring worldly goods.   They are but impediments on his way to greater glories.

He must follow his bidding to do the utmost good to help and aid the people on his way through his journey back to the stars, back to Source where he ultimately belongs.

Your true path is to follow your heart, your intuition, your inner guiding from self.

Yes, we regenerate.   We are constantly recreating.   We evolve and adapt which is the key to our survival."

ETCHINGHAM

ST. MARY & ST. NICHOLAS ASSUMPTION CHURCH, EAST SUSSEX

"Perseverance"

Interestingly, without even looking at the yews, I'm starting to instinctively know whether they are male or female. This yew is definitely male and I've been here a good few minutes trying to make contact but am beginning to wonder whether he's sleeping.

I'm torn between carrying on and disturbing him or to leave him to his slumber? Just as I'm about to leave him be, we finally connect. There is a strong "grandfather" feel and I get the distinct impression he should be smoking a pipe reclining in a chair by the fire!

YEW MESSAGE:

Gender: Male
Age: AD 498
Name: N/A

Me: [Hello... sorry are you resting?]

"Ach... I was not sleeping Little One, merely reminiscing. Reminiscing about times long ago, when you were just a speck of dust. Times were hard. The people were tough – as they had to be to survive. However, they lacked in spirituality and insight. They could only see as far as the next meal. Times are now different... and yet the same. Humans only seem able to focus on their own wants and needs for the immediate future. The majority do not look forward at the bigger picture.

Oh, that they could see the world from the stars, from the heavens. They would behold a glorious ray of energy, all around and in between. They would see the thin wisps of light beings that weave the matrix of All That Is around Everything That Is, giving it a purpose, a meaning. Sinews dancing in the wild, coating all that comes within their reach with a wondrous beauty of nature and heaven intertwined in the love of the Creator.

One day you will be able to see and behold the seamless energies that bind us all together and you will decree: behold! How was I not able to witness this before. Until that time, you must all strive to reach your inner purpose with clarity of vision which comes from listening to That Which Is Inside Of You. With perseverance comes all manner of delights."

"PEACE & HARMONY"

"Develop Awareness In

All That You Do"

"GENEROSITY OF SPIRIT"

"Practise Loving Kindness"

1998

I'm considering my options.

Typical Aquarian and being of an independent nature, it feels wrong to be relying on others for help. I quite like the idea of being able to self-heal, but this is out of my comfort zone and I'm struggling on where to start.

So far I've come up with the following options:-

Acupuncture: not easily self-administered, the training goes on forever and needles give me the heebie jeebies.

Kinesiology: not such a steep learning curve but still difficult to self-administer.

Reflexology: easier to do on myself and I know there are also pressure points relating to the energy meridians in the hands. However, not being particularly keen on feet the thought of training on someone else's leaves me feeling queasy.

Reiki: something I can do on myself, I don't have to touch anyone, not too difficult to learn and I enjoy the experience. Seems to fit all criteria, Reiki it is.

PETHAM

ALL SAINT'S CHURCH, EAST SUSSEX

"Be In The Here & Now"

Now *that* was a very narrow country lane I've just had to negotiate… and breathe!!

Finding the lane was a mission in itself but I'm more than made up with finding this happy chappy who's cheerful uplifting energy has definitely raised my spirits.

He's also given me a somewhat different, beautiful message to those I've received from the others so far…

YEW MESSAGE:

Gender: Male
Year: AD 411
Name: N/A

"Fear not for we have holy wings that allow us to soar through the skies on sheets of sun rays and feather like clouds of dew drops.

We are sailing through the sea of time.   An endless journey through life and love.

We seek to enjoy and have fun.

To frolic in the morning haze of life's bountiful harvest.

Life is for loving.   Life is for living.

Life is for being in the here and now, for there is no here and now as each moment that you taste is gone in the blink of an eye.   And that surely is indeed a conundrum!

Grab life with both hands... and feet if you dare!

Take advantage of each opportunity that presents to enjoy your life. Don't miss the chance to experience deep everlasting love, for love is the only thing that matters in the Universe."

ELMSTED [1]

ST. JAMES THE GREAT CHURCH, KENT

"Life's Lessons"

As usual, the sat-nav has decided the church at Elmsted is in the middle of a main road. Sighhhh. After stopping at a nearby pub, I've been directed down some meandering country lane that has had my heart in my mouth all the way. The hedgerows are so high it's impossible to see round the corners so I'm driving at a snails pace and fervently praying I don't meet a tractor coming towards me.

I do love our English countryside and whilst visiting the yews I've been to some of the most picturesque villages I would never have dreamed of visiting normally. However, I do SO hate navigating these narrow lanes.

YEW MESSAGE:

Gender: Male
Year: AD 239
Name: N/A

"My child... Little One... you are doing well to connect with all of us in such a short space of your time.

We have been around the world, figuratively speaking.

We are all in communication.   We share the world's joys and sorrows. We delight when your spirits are uplifted and feel tormented when you are experiencing great griefs.

Our hearts are here sharing in all of your life experiences and we pass these back to Source.   We are all learning and on the wheel of life. Where we go and end up depends on the nature and spirit of our hearts.

Even though we are but a blip in the grand scheme of things, all life experiences and learning count towards helping those who come after us and tread on the same path but with different footsteps.   Joy be to the world."

"FOLLOW YOUR HEART"

"Perseverance"

"BE IN THE HERE AND NOW"

"Life's Lessons"

2001

I've just had my Reiki Level 1 Attunement after which you (apparently) go through a 21 day cleanse where the body resets itself, re-aligns and balances to the new energies.

Maybe it's my analytical IT background, but I'm feeling kind of sceptical about the whole process — has anything actually happened??

A week or so later, I troll along to my monthly acupuncture session and wait patiently while Mark, my acupuncturist, 'reads the pulses' in my wrist so he knows what's unbalanced and needs working on.

He sits, eyes closed, reading my pulses for far longer than usual and I'm beginning to wonder if he's nodded off. Eventually he sits back and says with a puzzled expression "Sorry Paula, but I can't treat you today. For some reason, your pulses won't stay still long enough for me to read them. I've never encountered anything like it before!". Huh??

Mystified, we sit quizzically looking at each other. Ahhh... it eventually dawns on me to mention I've just had my Level 1 Reiki attunement. Doh!

"Well, that explains it!" he says, relieved.

This is the perfect confirmation I need that the Reiki energies are 'doing something'. I leave the session with a sense of intrigue as to what's in store (and interestingly, I've not required an acupuncture session since).

ELMSTED [2]

ST. JAMES THE GREAT CHURCH, KENT

"Observe"

There are two Ancients and two Veteran yews here and having taken my life in my hands along another narrow lane I know there's no way I'm going to be back here in a hurry.

I'm determined to get round and speak to them all so have planned on spending most of the day here. So much so, that I've brought something to eat and have plenty of water. To be honest, I'm more worried about depleting my energy levels than I am about going hungry.

I've noticed I'm usually on site for about an hour or so, wandering about taking pictures and getting the feel of the place before settling in to chat.

The days are starting to draw in and it's now mid-November, so hopefully the weather will hold and not get too chilly so I can give each tree justice with my time.

Yew Message:

Gender: Male
Year: AD 238
Name: N/A

"Yes, I know you.   I know who you are.   We have been watching your work.   The winds are our ears and the birds are our eyes... and the earth touches our soul.   We are consciousness personified in our workings with the land.   We are here to help and defend for those who will heed our calling and respect our very nature.   We lean towards the stars and bathe in the moons' glorious light... and we observe and listen.

Wait!!... [I was about to leave]... We drink in all that is going on around, oblivious to any of mankind.

We note the pleasures and displeasure of those who visit this place and strive to shed illumination for those who are able to listen and heed our call.   Be observant to those around who are in need of help.".

ELMSTED
[VETERAN 1]
ST. JAMES THE GREAT CHURCH, KENT

"Treat The Earth & Air With Respect"

Elmsted Ancients ticked off the list, I'm on a roll and onto the Veterans. The shape of this yew really appeals to me for some reason, although he has a fairly sobering message which, to me, seems at odds with his form.

YEW MESSAGE:

Gender: Male
Age: AD 1361
Name: N/A

"We do not judge, we merely observe the energy of all living creatures. My words and messages are carried on the air that we breathe.

The air which cleanses our souls and nourishes the blood that courses through our veins. We too have blood, though it's different indeed from your own. We cry and hurt when we are cut, yet we heal and bear the wounds with pride.

Mankind must treat the earth and air around us with respect, for without their nourishment we would all cease to be. Ancient Ones included. No matter how hard we try to regenerate, we would not withstand a contaminated environment.

You have the power within you all to make this world a better, healthier place for all human kind. All should heed this warning lest we all suffer.

Blessings be to those on this planet who follow the path of righteousness. Strength and resilience to all who turn from the path of power and greed."

ELMSTED
[VETERAN 2]
ST. JAMES THE GREAT CHURCH, KENT

"Persistence Is The Key"

The second Veteran message is more light-heated than his brother and I'm rather glad I've now spoken to them all as, lovely as they are, I'm beginning to feel the cold and in need of warm sustenance. A hot chocolate is beckoning!

YEW MESSAGE:

Gender: Male
Year: AD 1396
Name: N/A

"It is indeed my honour to give you a message for your brothers and sisters.

You are all blessed to be walking here at this time. It is a great time for change and holds many challenges for you all. However, persistence is the key to pushing through to the other side and, yes, there is indeed light at the other end. Glorious, radiant light that is waiting to bathe you all in its loving rays."

"OBSERVE"

"Treat The Earth & Air With Respect"

"PERSISTENCE IS THE KEY"

January 2002

I'm fidgeting on a seat in a village hall. It's a cold icy evening in January and, although curious, I'm wondering if this is such a good idea. Mum is sitting next to me and we're waiting for a clairvoyant to appear. Not knowing what to expect I'm starting to feel apprehension creeping in.

Everyone settles, all goes quiet and an elderly, affable chap appears. He gives a general introduction and relays an (apparently) accurate message from 'spirit' to a lady behind us.

He starts staring intently at me. Oh oh, I can feel myself flushing red with embarrassment. My great-grandmother is suddenly giving me advice on something only I could know. Er... how?

Not yet done, he turns to mum and starts talking to her about a Japanese flag my granddad's platoon had retrieved after an armed combat in Burma during the war. It seems they had all signed it and mum now has it.

First I've heard of any flag? I look at mum. She's nodding her head. We're both speechless.

BUXTED

CHURCH OF ST. MARGARET THE QUEEN OF SCOTLAND, EAST SUSSEX

"Peace To The World"

Set in stunning parkland with amazing views this is a beautiful location to spend an afternoon and I particularly love the shape of this yew, it reminds me of one of the Elmsted Veterans.

Conversation over, I'm rummaging around in the church and have found a document that says *"the yew tree at the east end of the church is more than 2,000 years old, but is still so vigorous that some 800 cuttings were taken and grown into little trees which were distributed all over the country as a millennium project."* What a splendid enterprise!

YEW MESSAGE:

Gender: Female
Age: 353 BC
Name: N/A

"Yes, you have patience Little One... but not as much as we do.

Our patience is beyond the measure of the stars.

We are acutely listening to the joys and woes of mankind.

It would be good that we could do more than we do but, alas, the majority of you are not attuned into our vibrational wave lengths to hear our voices, our song.   For you to do this you must have faith that we are conscious... In fact all living things have a consciousness which you would tap if you were so inclined.

You must also be open to our words which not only appear in your own consciousness but in your heart.

Your soul will know whether this is familiar... And by that we mean familiar to your core, your inner being, your connection with the Universe.

Yes... I have Divas that attend to me.   They are always here... They protect against environmental stresses and keep me company.   Yes, we talk to each other... They have the gift of communicating in 'tree', which obviously is much easier for us than speaking to you in your native language which takes some effort.   But worthwhile and heartfelt, nonetheless...

Yes, that is why we oft struggle to find the correct wording to give you... Your language is unnatural to us but you would not be able to accurately report and interpret our emotions should we instil you with them.

I hope this has been useful to you and I take this opportunity to extend our blessings and hope for peace to the world."

CHAILEY

ST. PETER'S CHURCH, EAST SUSSEX

"Faith & Strength"

As with Elmsted, there is a Veteran yew just along the path from this Ancient and I'm quite taken aback with both of these messages. It would never have occurred to me the spiritual nature of the work the yews are performing on our behalf! They certainly give a fascinating insight into some of the reasons for their purpose and I'm wondering if this may help explain why most of their essence is toxic...?

YEW MESSAGE:

Gender:	Male
Year:	AD 675
Name:	N/A

"I have been waiting for you and yes, I have known of your coming - I was told. I have been preparing for you and practising my language skills! I may not be as adept as some of my brothers but I will do my best.

In the far off, distant times past, we were put here to ward off evil or bad, no let's just call them 'unkindly' spirits, from your world. The best way of describing it to you is that we soak them up, or absorb them. This is why we are toxious* to other beings.

We contain the essence of the 'unfriendly' that have gone before... and still yet appear. We do our best to envelop them in our love and hold them dear. Our hope is that when they have learned that there is more to being than, let's call it 'fear', we can lovingly release them back into the ether in the hope they can pass on their lessons to others they might encounter along the way.

This is not our only purpose but one we take with great care and dedication. Our message to you this day is to keep strong and keep your faith that the world is improving, even if it seems just ever so slightly. Faith and strength be your friends my Little One."

*For those puritans out there, yes, "toxious" isn't actually an English word, however that is what he said, so I've left it in.

CHAILEY
[VETERAN]
ST. PETER'S CHURCH, EAST SUSSEX

"Look At The Stillness Of Time & Space"

This Veteran is Just along the path and, unsurprisingly, his message is in the same vein to that of his brother.

YEW MESSAGE:

Gender: Male
Year: AD 1057
Name: N/A

"We strive to, no... We endeavour... To produce more love in the world by taking away the impurities that would cause the lesser mortals to stray from their chosen paths.

We do this in a gentle way and with the permission and cooperation of the spirit that finds its way into our presence.

We do not force and we do not coerce.   We merely show and explain a different way of being, of looking at the stillness of time and space and how to survive and grow spiritually.

These are fallen spirits who have found their way to us and not yet made it to the doorway of light that is their rightful inheritance.

They may abide with us for only a short time or they may take refuge and be comforted until they feel strong enough to venture out and into the tunnel of light that awaits them.

My love and blessings are with you all on this glorious day."

"PEACE TO THE WORLD"

"Faith & Strength"

"LOOK AT THE STILLNESS OF

TIME & SPACE"

March 2002

The clairvoyant experience has ignited a sceptic interest and I'm struggling, but determined, to keep an open mind.

To this end, I'm sitting surrounded by a pile of books on spirituality.

Where to start; spirit messages from medium Doris Stokes... Angel books by Diana Cooper... The Celestine Prophecy by James Redfield... Conversations with God by Neale Donald Walsch. A veritable Pandora's box of goodies!

Having hungrily devoured all the above (and more) I'm starting to get drawn into the whole spiritual concept. Fascinated, I'm having to restrain myself from boring everyone to death (no pun intended) on the whole 'energy thing'.

I'm also discovering not everyone is too impressed with the idea of angels and think I've lost the plot. Being described as "woo-woo" is something I'm obviously going to have to get used to.

ROTHERFIELD
ST. DENYS CHURCH, EAST SUSSEX

"Love Your Fellow Man"

It's a couple of weeks since I was at Chailey and it's now mid-December. How quickly the weather can turn from one week to the next. Despite being wrapped up to the nines, it's getting a bit cold to be standing in one spot, so I have a feeling this may be the last yew I'll be speaking to for a while.

Unlike most of the other yews I've visited, the churchyard where this Ancient resides is in the middle of the village. Not what I was expecting and I almost drove straight past it. I've parked on the main road and keep furtively looking about hoping no-one walking past will question what I'm up to.

Despite being supported with poles and most of the trunk having disappeared years ago, this yew is in good humour and sounds quite resilient.

Literature in the church believes the yew to be over 1500 years old. Sadly, he feels himself to be in poor health due to the level of cleansing and nurturing of spirit he's performed over the years.

YEW MESSAGE:

Gender: Male
Year: AD 248
Name: N/A

"Find peace and tranquillity in your heart to hear my words for I know it is cold.   You have travelled far to hear my words so I hope my message may be of benefit.   It is with joy that I have to say how wonderful the human race can be.   They are a blessing to the world and have it in their hearts to hold peace and goodwill.   They will find it within them to be uplifting to those around who would stumble and fall.   It may take some time for this to happen, but happen it will as it is your destiny to be loving and peaceful to your fellow man.

This is the time of year you humans celebrate the passing of Christ, therefore may you find extra time to dwell on those around who are not so fortunate to be able to celebrate the peace and goodness of others. Joy be to all.

... I was placed here to be a beacon of light to those who dwelled in nearby surroundings.   People flocked to me to celebrate their ancient rituals of honouring the earth.   Alas, I was in better strength then, but I am not done wassailing yet!"

CROWHURST

ST. GEORGE'S CHURCH, SURREY

"Find Peace Within & With Nature"

It's now the beginning of the Summer and what a beautiful spot to spend an afternoon! The church looks and feels almost as old as the yew.

This Ancient has such a lovely soft, wise, calming voice. I feel as though I should be addressing him as 'Your Majesty' and curtseying to royalty.

So... I've been chatting with the yew for a while and we've just gone through the process of testing how old he is. I'm a bit stunned to be honest and beginning to think I've definitely lost my marbles or failing dismally at working out their ages. He reckons he's over **5,000** years old...?!

Still questioning my intuition, I've ambled into the church and would you believe, have discovered a document proclaiming the tree to be 4,000 years old!! It seems the naturalist David Bellamy authenticated his age during the Yew Tree Campaign in 1989. I'm still a bit stunned but now gratified and exhilarated that intuition hasn't totally failed me.

The document also notes that he was hollowed out in 1820, fitted with a door (which can still be seen) and inside with a table and bench that could fit 12 people.   I find that quite sad and in retrospect slightly regret not having asked how he felt about that.

YEW MESSAGE:

Gender: Male
Year: 3364 BC
Name: N/A

[Clearing throat]… *"It has been a long time since I talked to anyone so please forgive me if my words do not come easily or naturally.*

It feels as though I have been here since before time began and certainly before humans inhabited this part of the world.

I have been at peace and I am still at peace.   There is lots of peace in this world still to be had - believe it or not!   You humans search for peace externally, but peace is to be found within.   Within and with nature.

You do not take time to stop and listen to the joyful noises around you. Appreciate nature in all its beauty.

When you stop and take time to appreciate the beauty of nature you will find peace in your hearts, even if just for a fleeting moment.   You will treasure the feeling and your body will remember… your mind will still and your body energies will align to the energy of the nature around you.   This is peace.   This is joy.   This is being at one with yourself and all around you.

Those of you who live life at a frenetic pace are missing the joys and blessings this world has to offer.

Beauty is not in the eyes of the beholder – it is within and all around us. If only you would take the time to open your eyes and behold, you would cherish life more and be more at one with the Universe and all energy beings.

Thank you for coming here today Little One, you have brightened my soul to be able to express my thoughts into words that may help bring joy and peace to your kind."

ADDITIONAL DIALOGUE:

After finding the document inside the church I've come back to the yew to see why he thinks he's older than reported:-

[Me:] *"You are alleged to be 4,000 years old and yet you believe yourself to be over 5,000?"*

"There was a period of intense cold. I went into hibernation - for survival. I slept for a long time to conserve energy. It is not unknown for trees to adopt this pattern during times of intense stress."

[Me:] Thank you for chatting with me today. It has been a joy and a privilege and I hope your words will one day spread across the world like ripples across the ocean.

2003

A new world is opening up for me.

I must have traipsed along to every holistic and psychic fayre going. My house is so full of crystals I could open a shop!

This whole clairvoyant, spiritual curiosity has gripped me. I'm enthralled. I've lost count of the number of tarot/angel readings I've been given and the fascinating clairvoyant evenings I've attended. Messages have been relayed from my great-grandmother, great-grandfather, my grandfather and my aunt. I never know what to expect and each evening is always full of surprises, sparking my intrigue more deeply.

I'm beginning to ponder whether there's something I could do to explore and develop my own intuitive abilities and learn how to tap into them. I'm still doing Reiki, regularly practise T'ai Chi and am familiar with the chakras (the body's energy system) but somehow that doesn't feel quite enough.

TANDRIDGE

ST. PETER'S CHURCH, SURREY

"Cherish Each Other"

To explain the first part of our dialogue; notices inside the church and around the yew ask visitors to respect its age and not walk near the roots. Interesting. It's the first time I've seen such a request so I positioned myself a bit further back under one of his long branches and asked if it was OK to stand there.

I know this yew is male, except... When I tune in, the energy has a feminine quality to it. So I ask for clarification and am definitely put in my place when he scolds: *"I'm a young male you silly girl"*...!

Despite our inauspicious start, he is lovely and full of vigour.

YEW MESSAGE:

Gender: Male
Year: AD 132
Name: N/A

"We have foreseen your coming.   You are talked about on the breeze. It will take more than your light footsteps to harm my root system – I have been here for hundreds of years and my roots go deep!"

[Me:] *"Do you have a message that would help humanity?"*

"Yes!! Love one another!! Love each other with every ounce of your being... Like you've never loved anything more on this planet.

LOVE WITH EVERY BREATH... With every fibre of your soul... With all your heart.   Love is all there is... Love begets love... Love and you will be loved in return.

There is nothing more important in this world than to love everyone and everything.

Your mission is to go out into this world and spread the love.

There is no more message as important than reminding people to cherish each other."

TANDRIDGE
[VETERAN]
ST. PETER'S CHURCH, SURREY

"BE Love"

Both the Ancient and Veteran yews at Tandridge talk about either spreading love or being love and, rather curiously, they both have a very similar limb structure.

YEW MESSAGE:

Gender: Male
Year: AD 1229
Name: N/A

"I am happy to share my words with the world but I fear they may not be as wise as some of those from my counterparts with whom you've been speaking...

Humans would benefit from hearing from so much, but alas they only hear what they want to hear.

If they could lighten their hearts and lift their eyes to the heavens they would behold so much goodness that is around them.

They would sing together as a choir of angels, telling all of the light and love they can see.

For indeed, they are surrounded by light and love from all other beings and it is a strange, sad thing that they are oblivious to the wondrous rays of love and energy that surround them.

Not only is it a gift to extend light and love, it is your birthright.

You are all beautiful in the eyes of God, the Universe and Nature.

Stand tall... be proud... BE love".

"LOVE YOUR FELLOW MAN"

"Find Peace Within & With Nature"

"CHERISH EACH OTHER"

"Be Love"

2004

It's said that people come into your life when you need them or when appropriate.

Enter Avis.

While attending a clairvoyant demonstration this evening I've been introduced to Avis. A most extraordinary medium with a heart of gold. It seems she runs a spiritual development circle and I've been invited to join the weekly sessions.

I'm always eager to explore and experience new concepts and, who knows, it might help me learn how to increase my awareness, improve my intuition and possibly even connect with the spiritual realm. I can feel bubbles of excitement!

KENNINGTON

ST. MARY'S CHURCH, KENT

"Love All Beings"

You'll notice that for the first time I have a tree name!*

On the spur of the moment, it occurred to me to ask if their tree name could be translated, how I wish that thought had popped into my head months ago.

The church here is very old and quaint but sadly (and unusually), is locked.

YEW MESSAGE:

Gender:	Male
Year:	AD 729
Name:	'Merciful'

[Me:]   Hello? Are you there?

"Oh, I am here Little One..."

[Me:]   Would you mind talking to me for a while?

"I will do my best, what would you like to know?

[Me:]   I was wondering if you have a message for humanity?

Hmm.. that's quite a big subject – where to start!   There are any number of areas which would benefit mankind to pay more attention to, however the one that would befit all to remember is to cherish one another.

Love all beings... and that includes all living beings, whether or not in human form.

I have seen all manner of things over time, from destruction to kindness and empathy.   From nature and emptiness to civilisation appearing. And there is neither better or worse, good or bad about either, as long as man can align himself with the qualities of nature and the higher good of all."

[Me:]   Thank you Great One

"My pleasure Little One.   It has been a joy talking to you today and may our messages reach the Intended Ones."

[Me:]   If I could translate your name into English, what would be the closest translation?

"Merciful"

* The names of the yews at Crowhurst, East Sussex were established during a subsequent visit.

KENNINGTON VETERAN [1]

ST. MARY'S CHURCH, KENT

"Ignorance Needs To Change"

I always ask the yews if they're able to impart any messages of wisdom for humanity. The message of love, cherishing other beings and being in nature is beginning to feel like a standard theme.

YEW MESSAGE:

Gender: Female
Year: AD 977
Name: 'Mindfulness'

"I have heard you talking to my brother.."

[I'm being distracted by the smell of fox poop and millions of ants]

"Yes... I am visited by a lot of foxes and there are always ants. Always.

So, you would like to tap into my wisdom for humanity hmm?   As my fellow spirit said, that is a difficult one.

However, I believe it is crucial that mankind work with one another for the greater good of the planet.   There is too much decay and destruction of our natural resources.

Man is destroying Mother Earth, as you humans refer to her. She is a gift to you all and has an abundance of wealth to offer. However there are areas of ignorance that remain on this planet which need to change before you destroy the habitat for all to follow after humans have ceased to be.

Planet earth is neither male or female although there is an aura of genteelness about it, an energy pattern which is more strongly linked to female energies."

"LOVE ALL BEINGS"

"Ignorance Needs

To Change"

2005

I completed my Reiki Level 2 a year ago and have been 'sitting in circle' for some time now.

With Avis's help, I've learnt how to communicate with my main Spirit Guide – Sister Claire. A sprightly Mother Superior in her dotage with round spectacles who often appears dancing and twirling through the stars! Sometimes she's in a white habit and others in dark blue.

I've managed to ascertain we had a past life together in Ireland. It seems I was taken in as an orphan and helped tend the kitchen garden.

I've also been given vivid images of the church interior with tall gothic stained glass windows and the stark room in a building nearby where my sleeping quarters were. A narrow slit window is casting a dingy light across cold stone walls revealing a basic sleeping ledge with a greyish-brown threadbare wool blanket and a small low three-legged stool.

Curiosity piqued once again, I'm wondering how easy it might be to investigate other past lives?

KENNINGTON
VETERAN [2]
ST. MARY'S CHURCH, KENT

"Halt The Level Of Hatred"

The church is across the road from a field and my concentration and patience are being sorely tested.

It's such a warm day I'm being attacked by a zillion small flies who must think it'll be a fun game to try and crawl into the slightest crack in my attire or down my neck...

YEW MESSAGE:

Gender: Male
Year: AD 963
Name: 'Awareness'

"Please forgive the ants and insects, they are doing nature's work.

My message to you today is to tell your people to halt the level of hatred towards each other.

It is time to stop the feelings of negativity and greed for power.

You all have such a short span of life here on this planet that surely it is better to work as one brethren for the betterment of all and the enjoyment of every being."

KENNINGTON
VETERAN [3]
ST. MARY'S CHURCH, KENT

"Persevere"

It's taken a while to connect to this yew and I've found the reason for the delay truly fascinating.

There are definitely times when I know a dialogue is over and they no longer wish to communicate.

That was the case in this instance, which is a shame as I would have liked to explore the notion of 'shape shifting' further.

YEW MESSAGE:

Gender: Male
Age: AD 965
Name: 'Thoughtfulness'

"Hello Little One… I am here, I am back… sorry, I was on a different energy plane and could hardly hear you".

[Me:]   What do you mean?

"Like you, we are beings of energy and although our physical form is that of a tree, we can travel to different energy planes to learn and discover new ways or alternate ways of thinking.

Our thought process may be different from yours and one that you would have a tough time understanding, nevertheless we are sentient beings and our evolution and enlightenment continues.

I ask that mankind persevere in its efforts to progress and evolve into the light.

To be able to shape shift from one world to another at will whilst remaining in your physical form here on this planet will expand your thoughts and ways of perceiving that which you have not yet conquered in terms of lightness of spirit to yourself and towards your fellow man."

"HALT THE LEVEL

OF HATRED"

"Persevere"

2006

One of the most precious aspects of developing my psychic abilities has been to be able to connect with loved ones who have passed.

Having said that, there have been times when communicating with 'the other side' is both a blessing and a challenge.

One day, my little 'wind-up' alarm clock started to go off at 3.20 am. Initially, I put it down to having set it incorrectly. When it then happened several more times I thought it was my daughter playing a joke. However, it then started occurring on a regular basis when she wasn't even in the house. Something odd was happening...

It took a while before it finally dawned on me, my Granddad died at 3.20am and this must be his way of saying hello!

Following many one-on-one mentoring sessions with Avis I was finally able to telepathically communicate with him and the early morning wake up calls abated. However, one night a couple of years later, after setting the burglar alarm, sure enough, at 3.20am the alarm went off frightening the living daylights out of me!!

MOLASH [1]

ST. PETER'S CHURCH, KENT

"Develop Your Skills"

There are no less than six yews on this site and records apparently indicate a seventh which is now lost. I've decided to stretch myself and see if I can manage to talk to all six in one day.

Strictly speaking, three Ancients and three Veterans are registered at this site, however according to how old the yews believe themselves to be and the overlap between Ancient/Veteran, I've decided to include them all as Ancients.

The church is in the heart of the countryside surrounded by fields and for the second time in a row it's locked.

I think the fields must have just been harvested as there are millions of tiny, irritating, black thunder flies everywhere. I'm reminded of Kennington and my heart sinks. Hopefully, I can withstand the onslaught and not let it interrupt my conversations.

I've also noticed there's a bundle of white feathers around the base of the tree. My initial thoughts are that an unfortunate bird was the midnight snack for a fox. However, on closer inspection I can see there are little piles of white feathers around the base of each of the yews, as if someone has deliberately placed them. How odd.

YEW MESSAGE:

Gender: Male
Year: AD 1129
Name: 'Altruistic'

[Me:] I feel as though I'm being scanned...!

"Ha-ha.. yes you are being scanned and your heart is pure although you are finding it difficult to tolerate the ants I see.

Well now... there is a time and place for everything and everyone.

It is humanity's time to be here on this earth plane at this moment.

You are here to preserve the planet and to develop your skills as earth workers with light in your hearts that you are able to use to promote peace and world healing.

You have a duty of care to help enrich the planet you live on."

MOLASH [2]

ST. PETER'S CHURCH, KENT

"Tap Into Your Inner Energies"

Interestingly, the yews refer to themselves as being in 'fixed form' and humans as in 'physical form' yet, unlike us humans, they don't have amnesia when they re-incarnate.

I've particularly enjoyed this conversation as it's delivered fascinating new insights into the differences between our incarnations.

YEW MESSAGE:

Gender: Male
Year: AD 365
Name: 'Benevolence'

"Welcome Little One, welcome to my home.

It is an honour to finally talk with you. We have heard of your intention to relay our words to the Universe and we are happy to oblige. May it be that the recipients heed our messages and honour our intent.

Trees have stood for millennia on this earth ball and we have learned great things and a great deal of our learning has been passed down from century to century.

We have our own paths to follow, as do you, and our messages may be hard to take on board as we are of fixed form and do not possess the physical agility of humans. However, we are also beings of light and can skip through the spiritual planes as can you, therefore we are not so far apart.

However, I believe we are more advanced in our ability to transfer information from one generation to another without fear of loss of memory and can recollect at will that which has been given to us.

If you can, tap into your inner memories, that would serve you well."

MOLASH [3]

ST. PETER'S CHURCH, KENT

"Appreciate The Energies Of Others"

This yew also makes reference to our different forms and it's interesting to note how we all chose which form we wanted through every incarnation.

YEW MESSAGE:

Gender: Male
Age: 256 BC
Name: 'Fearsome'

"Focus Little One..." [I've been momentarily distracted watching a woodlouse]... *"We are all here in spirit together.*

We share the same energy source and in The Beginning we all chose the path we wanted to follow and the form we wanted to take through each life time. We were fully aware of the pitfalls involved in our choices and of the delights that could also await us.

It is heartening that many of your life forms have taken the unprecedented decision to attempt to communicate with beings on a different spiritual path.

It is always useful to appreciate the energies of others."

MOLASH [4]

ST. PETER'S CHURCH, KENT

"Transfer Your Achievements"

I'm just loving some of the names these yews have!

YEW MESSAGE:

Gender: Male
Year: 174 BC
Name: 'Dodecahedron'

"My message would be similar to those of my kin.

We all chose a different course when we were being honoured with the Gift of Light.   Both beings have had different issues to contend with. Ours are no more easier or difficult than yours, they are just different, with different skill sets and spiritual lessons to absorb.

I would choose the same life form again should I be given another choice as it has much to offer in terms of spiritual enlightenment and species evolution.

May you be able to learn to transfer and pass on your achievements to future generations."

2007

I've ventured into a new area – the angelic realm!

A lovely lady by the name of Karen is able to channel these amazing beings and I've been attending her weekly angel workshops.

Not only have we been able to enjoy angel messages but have also been learning how to connect with the Ascended Masters, our Guardian Angel and our Higher Self.

The more work I do with the angelic beings the more I'm drawn to angel energy than that of spirit. As much as I love talking to spirit and family members who have passed, I think it may be because the angelic energies feel so much lighter and more loving.

The sessions have also reminded me of a time a few years ago when my Guardian Angel, a beautiful golden being, appeared in a nightmare one evening and enfolded me in her wings. White feathers often indicate angelic presence and the following morning an enormous white feather lay on the floor by the side of the bed.

MOLASH [5]

ST. PETER'S CHURCH, KENT

"Spiritual Connection"

To explain the first part of our dialogue I asked this 'Friendly Giant' why there aren't so many female yews.

YEW MESSAGE:

Gender: Male
Year: AD 926
Name: 'Friendly Giant'

"A lot of females do not make it through harsh climate changes."

[... commenting on how he's classed as a Veteran]

"Aye... Not far off being classed as an Ancient One in your terminology. However, we see all beings as special and unique, each possessing different qualities of beauty and richness. We communicate effortlessly and have mastered the art of spiritual connection in our energy fields. You have not yet accomplished this and are still struggling in your efforts

to communicate effectively with each other.

This would be a great leap for mankind and it is an area you would do well to focus your attention on."

MOLASH [6]
ST. PETER'S CHURCH, KENT

"Welcome All Forms Of Learning"

This is my last tree here at Molash and, quite frankly, I can't wait to finish.

Not very spiritual I know, however I'm being bitten to death and finding small black flies everywhere. After several hours of being on the fly 'hit list' I'm ready for home!

YEW MESSAGE:

Gender: Male
Year: AD 844
Name: 'Delightful'

[Me:] You are debating whether to talk to me?

"Yes, I am, I am wondering whether there is too much distraction in all the flying insects that seem to be in force today. "

[I confess, despite my most concerted efforts, I *am* struggling to retain concentration, continually having to stop and flick off masses of wriggling flies... However, this is the last tree and I'm not about to give up just yet!]

"Although our skin is sensitive, I appreciate it is nothing as sensitive as yours and I am sorry you are being set upon. The tiny insects are attracted to the light. Any light, which includes all spiritual beings.

My message to you is to welcome with open arms all forms of learning that will help you on your path, wherever the path may lead.

May you find joy and laughter on the path, else it will be a long road and one of an exceedingly dark night."

"DEVELOP YOUR SKILLS"

"Tap Into Your Inner Energies"

"APPRECIATE THE
ENERGIES OF OTHERS"

"Transfer Your Achievements"

"SPIRITUAL CONNECTION"

"Welcome All Forms Of Learning"

2010

A small group of us who shared our Reiki 2 and Reiki Masters journey have formed a strong energetic bond and friendship. We meet once a week to meditate, explore new ideas and perform group healing. This weekend we've all enrolled in a 'tapping' course, also known as the Emotional Freedom Technique (EFT).

It's a technique I've often seen Paul McKenna, the hypnotherapist, use so I'm curious to see how it might help relieve symptoms a negative experience or emotion may have caused.

The idea is that by tapping on certain meridian points (similar to acupressure) whilst repeating a set of statements it's possible to restore balance to the body's energy.

An interesting and emotional weekend, in more ways than one, which I think we all experienced. I can certainly see the benefits although feel slightly daunted at being able to construct the appropriate tapping statements. As with all things, I guess practise makes perfect,

ULCOMBE [1]

ALL SAINT'S CHURCH, KENT

"Spend More Time In Nature"

There are two Ancients, a Veteran and a Notable at this church and thankfully I'm starting to get into the swing of being able to conserve my energy to talk to several in one day.

Peeping surreptitiously round the trunk, I can see the verger bobbing about, so I duck back a bit further and am going to do my best to keep a low profile.

It can be a tad awkward when I'm spotted standing with my hands on a tree trunk motionless for a while. Don't want to be carted away just yet!

YEW MESSAGE:

Gender: Male
Year: 433 BC
Name: 'Huggable'

"Hello Little One. How are you today?"

[Me:]   Very well thank you and how are you?

"I am in rude health!"

[Me:]   You seem very cheerful!

"Of course, what is there not to be cheerful about. The seasons are always kind to me these days and nature itself is a wonder to behold, especially when you are able to see for miles around. As my brother said, nature is a wondrous thing and it would behove you all to spend more time in her splendiferous arms!

You are like specs of dust in the time span of this world and the most you can take from it the better and easier your next lifetime will become. That of course, is not always the case but in the main you humans and indeed, all living beings, grow with each passing."

[Me:]   Why do yews split down the middle?

"It is like a human calcification of the bones. Our centre core ages faster than our outer limbs and starts to decay over time, seizing up with age. However, we have learned to produce new limbs and in this way we are able to preserve the essence of our self that once was the foundation of whence we came."

[Me:]   Is it painful to experience this regrowth?

"No, it is invigorating to have young blood run through our veins once again. It fills our inner self with love and gratitude."

ULCOMBE [2]
ALL SAINT'S CHURCH, KENT

"Spread The Word"

As usual, I've scoured the church looking for information on the yews and have come across a notice that states a cutting was taken from this yew in 1999 which is flourishing nicely next to it.

In quite a lot of the churches the yews have been placed in each corner of the churchyard. This church is no exception and I asked why this is the case.

YEW MESSAGE:

Gender: Male
Year: 528 BC
Name: 'Hallelujah'

"Hello Little One, please excuse my tardiness, I was elsewhere.

What may I assist with today?

I sense I'm expected to be saying something profound and deep, however instead I shall tell you all to go to the top of the highest mountain and sing as loud as you can. Jump, yell and shout to the heavens as to how happy and joyous you are to be living at this magnificent time on this earth plane.

It is a blessing and a privilege that we are here in these times.

You have the opportunity to turn around and resolve some of the wrongdoings of your predecessors and make good for generations to come. There, would you know, I lapsed into profundity after all, ha ha!

These are times for a period of rebirth and it is down to the light leaders to spread the word and do the work of The Universe for man to be at peace and loving towards each other once more. It has been too long since we walked the earth planes as One. Oh yes... We are entwined beneath the ground and our root system is as one still. Appearances are not all they seem and we are still joined.

[Me:]   Why do yews seem to be in four corners of a churchyard?

"Yews were placed in four corners for protection by the Ancients who would use the area for worship and rituals. They were more tuned into their energetic abilities than you are today and they were aware that we have the ability to soak up and cleanse any evil spirit, although I hesitate to use that word as nothing is evil, just misguided."

"SPEND MORE TIME
IN NATURE"

"Spread The Word"

2011

When was your last 'light bulb' or 'aha' moment?

One day you're busying away in the middle of something and the next moment 'boom', a life transforming thought occurs making you pause for breath.

A friend of mine mentioned in passing that she is going to enrol in a hypnotherapy course. A few days later and I'm in the shower enjoying the hot water pummelling my shoulders when the idea of also learning to become a hypnotherapist suddenly pops into mind, completely out of the blue.

Attending a University course I suppose I should have been prepared for degree level essays and exams. I definitely wasn't. Doing regimented essay work is something I struggle with and, maybe naively, I'd been expecting it to be an experiential learning experience. I'm always fascinated by synchronicity and when Ursula James' name kept appearing everywhere (who I'd never heard of before and later discovered she used to run the Uni course I'd just finished) it seemed appropriate to do a further year studying with her.

The mind is such a fascinating beast with so many hidden depths. Of all the different hypnotherapy sessions I've conducted over the years my favourite therapy is undoubtedly past life regression. The farthest any client has ventured back (so far!) is to the Cretaceous period. Only a mere 66 - 145 million years ago! Love it.

ULCOMBE
[VETERAN]
ALL SAINT'S CHURCH, KENT

"Be Outside"

This yew is officially classed as a Veteran, however he appears to be a lot older and, to my mind, should be classed as an Ancient, which he certainly feels.

During my conversations I periodically stop and note on my phone what is being said as there's absolutely no way I'd remember even half of our chats otherwise.

They don't have a problem with this and are happy to stop mid-flow waiting for me to catch up, the only proviso being that I don't place the phone against the trunk or any of the limbs as they don't like the energy that's emitted.

YEW MESSAGE:

Gender: Male
Age: AD 243
Name: 'Delectable'

"I am an old veteran... I have been here for many years and I feel weary. I am in good health but that doesn't stop the bones or "branches" from feeling tired.

This is a good resting spot. I have been happy here and I have been treated with respect from the local parishioners.

Where would you be without the art of technology? You are able to record my words on your small device and it is indeed a miracle that such things have come to pass.

Sadly, I think you humans are relying too much on power based objects and missing out on life itself.

The young and elderly are no longer taking in the beauty of the landscape around you.

You stagnate inside your boxes and do not get out and enjoy the natural wonders of this world.

There is much beauty to behold in even the smallest of nature's creatures and much they can teach you with regards to tolerance and perseverance.

My message to the world is to be outside in the gardens of the Universe".

ULCOMBE
[NOTABLE]
ALL SAINT'S CHURCH, KENT

"Revere All Life"

The verger seems to have disappeared so I come out of hiding in the bushes and creep through the undergrowth to get to this notable.

This is the first Notable I've spoken to, although he doesn't seem to have as much to say as his brothers. Maybe it's an age thing?

YEW MESSAGE:

Gender: Male
Year: AD 1454
Name: 'Sprightly

"Revere all life as it is more precious than you all appreciate.

You have the abilities to live a full and verdant life, with a purpose that is kind of heart and a nature that is loving and peaceful.

You are all aware of these facts but for some reason you choose to ignore and travel a path less smooth."

November 2012

Have you ever heard of the 'Balance Procedure'?

No, our Reiki group hadn't either so we decided to enrol on a workshop to discover more. It's a simple technique, the idea of which is to help restore/create centre and balance in all areas of life, to add a bit of 'magic' or 'sparkle'.

Devised by Jenny Cox (who has trained in everything imaginable) it has evolved from her work over the years using energy and meridian techniques and utilises a set of cards, each with different attributes and affirmations.

Without getting too technical, it utilises the heart chakra, which corresponds to the thymus on a physical level, which in turn communicates with the brain.

Anyway, holding the cards with your hand on your heart, if you then mentally ask a question the body will either sway forwards or backwards. For me, forwards is always a "yes" and backwards a "no", but it's always worth asking a simple question first to determine which way works for you (e.g. "is water good for me").

The sceptic in me struggled with the concept as it seems too easy. However, having completed the course I have to admit I'm impressed with the results (so long as the question is not ambiguous and only a 'yes' or 'no' being a possible answer!).

HARRIETSHAM

ST. JOHN THE BAPTIST CHURCH, KENT

"Peace To The World"

The outlook from the back of this church is simply beautiful.   Okay, so it may seem a bit odd for some to enjoy spending time in a graveyard, however it's a warm July day and I spy an inviting bench positioned just in front of the Veteran yew.

Before heading back into the hustle and bustle of the world I wander over and sit for a while enjoying the peace and calm. I can feel the warmth of the sun on my face and hear the birds twittering away. I don't think many of us spend enough time just 'being' which, when I pause to think about it, echoes what the yews keep telling us to do!

YEW MESSAGE:

Gender: Male
Age: AD 569
Name: 'Transformer'

"Welcome Little One, welcome to my place of rest.

It is a joy to finally meet and speak with you.   I have known for some time that you would be here and I was given word earlier that you were in the vicinity.

My message for mankind is the same as that of my kin, to be kind and cherish each other.   We are beginning to repeat ourselves now I think."

[Me:]   Do you spend much time in the spiritual planes?

We probably spend 50/50 between being focused in our physical form and the rest on our spiritual travels.   It is good to do both.   On the one hand we are surely well grounded and yet can also leave our fixed self and be away in our energetic field.   We have the best of all worlds I feel."

[Me:]   What do you think about when in fixed form?

"We ponder the beginning of time... We think about The Universe and how we may help those who are not yet here in order to prepare them for their forthcoming journey.

We meet our ancestors and obtain their words of wisdom that we might pass on."

[Me:]   What about any cleansing that you may do?

"Ah yes, that is another element of our work which, thankfully, hasn't been too large a task in this area of the country."

HARRIETSHAM
[VETERAN]
ST. JOHN THE BAPTIST CHURCH, KENT

"Learn To Co-Exist"

To date, I've been asking for a message for humanity, however the yews themselves have acknowledged they're all saying the same things, just dressed up a little differently.

So, recently I've started to ask a few questions to see if I can glean a bit more about what makes them 'tick'. With hindsight it would probably have made sense to compile a list rather than simply asking whatever springs to mind at the time!

YEW MESSAGE:

Gender: Male
Year: AD 1040
Name: 'Transcendence'

"Hello... I have been playing in the stars"

[Me:]   Oh, I'm really sorry to have disturbed you!

"It's no bother.   I can go back again easily enough"

[Me:]   What does it feel like to have sap and water move through your form?

"What does it feel like to have blood and water move through yours?   It is the same I think... neither of us are consciously aware but we both know it occurs.

In the same way I am not aware of insects that are on my bark, as you are not aware of the minute parasites you also harbour.   We co-exist."

[Me:]   How do trees deal with mankind logging them for wood?

"That is a tough one.   We are aware of their coming before they arrive and our fellow kind envelop us in their energetic embrace to sustain us and help our spirit transcend into the outer realms.

It is always a sad time but not one of grief as such, for we are acutely aware that our spiritual energy lives on whether we are physically present or not.   Humankind must learn to co-exist with each other and tolerate each others foibles and misdeeds."

October 2013

And... queue Kew (Gardens)

It's a damp, soggy day in October and I'm traipsing around Kew Gardens with a fellow tree-loving photographer friend. Accompanying us is a chap who was trying to chat her up on a recent flight back from our girls trip to Turkey. Not sure he is overly impressed I'm there, but hey ho!

While she's clicking away, I wonder if my Banyan conversation last year had been a fluke. So, wandering over to an Atlas Cedar I tentatively touch the bark and mentally ask if it has a message. I hear the following:

"When your heart feels heavy, dance as if you were full of joy to be uplifted".

Feeling delighted the energy connection is still there I slide about on wet leaves talking to as many different species of tree as I can, remembering this time to make notes on my phone.

Some are deciduous and slipping into a deep slumber. They aren't too keen on being disturbed and can only muster a brief message.

In retrospect, I feel guilty at having disturbed them, but at the time I was so elated at the prospect of still being able to communicate I couldn't resist.

Some of the messages received that day:-

Sweet Chestnut (300 years old according to a sign):
"Fly like the wind, soar above the stars, dream the sleep of the dead. When all around you is falling in chaos stand strong as though you were the eye in a storm".

Horse Chestnut:
"The old and the wise cannot compete with the young and the sprightly, however what we lack in physical ability we make up for with mental agility. Wear your years gracefully like a badge of honour."

Cork Oak sapling (my all time favourite):
"I want to skip through the hillsides in spring and make love in the morning dew with the passion of a sunset".

Hahaha!

I'm so astonished with this message I've asked him to repeat it just to be sure I've heard correctly!!

I'm laughing so much I've had to explain to the chap with us what I'm doing. He clearly thinks I'm bonkers!

BROOMFIELD

ST. MARGARET'S CHURCH, WEST SUSSEX

"Do Not Destroy The Planet"

I normally try and avoid any church 'official', however I've been spotted by the verger who is carefully mowing the grass and, to be fair, we've just had a lovely conversation. A cheerful chap, he stopped mowing as soon as he spied me. I think he was quite pleased to have someone to chat to and has spent a while regaling me with some of the church history.

Truthfully, I can't remember most of what he said apart from that it used to be the main church in the vicinity before the church at Leeds was built and, apart from weddings, is now only used once a month (the Vicar rotates round the local villages).

On a meander inside the church I've uncovered a document which states the yew is believed to be 1,000 years old which equates to how old he thinks he is.

YEW MESSAGE:

Gender: Male
Age: AD 887
Name: 'Formidable'

"Hello Little One."

(After exchanging all the usual pleasantries)

[Me:]   Can you feel the elements?

"Yes and no.   I can feel the element of wind as it makes my branches move, but I do not have the same sensitivity on my bark as you do on your skin."

(After asking for a message for humanity)

"My message is clear, do not destroy the planet.   Earth has survived for millennia and, although she will continue to do so long after you humans have vacated her, it would be gracious if you do not kill much of its inhabitants that are not in human form.

We are talking about the meek and the mild, if you like.   Those beings that are dependent on the health of the planet in order to survive.

The greed of man is unlimited and needs to be turned for the prevention of species extinction.

Unless man acts and puts his new found technology to good use, he will destroy much of the wildlife and habitat that you are still able to enjoy."

LEEDS

ST. NICHOLAS CHURCH, EAST SUSSEX

"More Respect"

This isn't the easiest of yews to gain access to and being so old his form has deteriorated to the degree that he needs to be held together with a fence.   That said, he doesn't sound particularly old!

YEW MESSAGE:

Gender: Male
Year: 354 BC
Name: 'Perseverance'

"You have come far, in terms of time and space.

It is no mean feat to be able to access our energy and tune into our vibrational field.

Our words can get confused and misinterpreted for random human thought. You have been given a gift few others receive and it is good to see you are trying to use this gift wisely.

We have been witness to countless human interchanges and humans still struggle to learn and appreciate the finer things that life has to offer them.

It is curious why it is taking your race so long to wake up to the call of life and to be able to honour and respect each other for who you are and not who you think each of you should be.

More respect is required for you to attain a higher evolution and longevity of life."

"BE OUTSIDE"

"Revere All Life"

"PEACE TO THE WORLD"

"Learn To Co-Exist"

"DO NOT DESTROY THE PLANET"

"More Respect"

November 2013

There are times when we deliberately give ourselves challenges, such as overcoming a fear. Other times challenges creep up on us unawares.

I've agreed to accompany a friend on a trip to Nepal and am high in the Himalayan mountains sitting in bed in a 'tea-house' perched on the side of a cliff. 'Bed' is an overstatement. The sleeping bag on the wooden platform is seriously too thin and it's freezing cold so our guide has organised a Yak blanket for me to spread over the top. Definitely 'yakk'. The smell is disgusting and I don't even want to contemplate what manner of icky-ness it's harbouring. The hut door doesn't properly close and when I lean back the corrugated sheet wall moves unnervingly, giving a glimpse of the drop to the valley floor below. It feels like I'm precariously balanced on the edge of a precipice. I ponder what on earth I'm doing here.

Day 2:
I've spent all day monotonously climbing 1200m of steep steps which have been carved into the mountain. It's blazingly hot, must be at least 30 degrees, and I'm carrying a loaded backpack. The jangling bells of ponies racing downhill signals everyone in their path to press in hard against the rock face to avoid being dislodged. Sticky and knackered we arrive at the tea lodge to discover there's no hot water left to shower - it's solar powered and we're late arriving. Sheesh. Can I manage 12 days of this?

After a seriously cold shower and much deliberating, my conscience gets the better of me. First, there's no way I can

133

abandon my mate and second, I feel a compelling need to see this through. I shall have to draw on inner strengths!

Day 3:

I'm clad in warm clothing including a thermal base layer, woolly hat, thick gloves and festooned with a head torch. I've just got up at 3am and climbed a rocky trail of steps up to 3200m to witness sunrise over the mountain range. As spectacular (and bloody freezing) as it is, did I seriously just do that?! Anyone who knows me will appreciate how NOT me this early morning climbing lark is!!

Day 10:

What must be (and certainly feels like) at least a 100 miles on and I'm a dress size smaller. I've even had to fashion my camera strap as a belt to stop my trousers from falling down as I walk. We've finally made it to Mountain Base Camp. It's well below zero and at 4200m above sea level, a struggle to breathe, but the landscape is breathtaking. Every time we thought about giving up and turning back our Sherpa said "nearly there, not long now". However, comfort in that thought fully evaporated when we then arrived at the half-way marker. One sheepish Sherpa...!

We've trekked through deserted rhododendron forests, navigated dodgy suspension bridges (shared with goats), gingerly stepped across landslides and jumped stones across icy rivers. Pretty cold and basic; we're sleeping fully clothed, including hats and gloves, and keeping everything crossed that we don't have to get up in the middle of the night to traipse to the outside hut masquerading as a toilet. Morning sees us breaking the ice off of the outside tap and standing huddled around it like emperor penguins to clean our teeth.

Day 12:

It's the end of the Annapurna trail and before returning to Kathmandu we're sitting lounging in the sun with a cold beer beside the lake at Pokhara. Gazing across the still water I'm lost in contemplation.

Naively, I'd assumed we'd be doing a straight ascent. So wrong! Up and down one steep valley onto the next, gradually winding our way up the mountain pass. Sometimes steps, others a rocky strewn trail or maybe over entangled twisted tree roots. We walked at our own pace and not being as fleet of foot as the Sherpa but faster than my mate, I often walked alone. Thankful of music to while away the long hours trudging up and down in the heat, my footsteps marched in time to the rhythms on my playlist.

Thankfully (and weirdly), every tea house we stopped at had internet. Everyone would charge their phones and various electrical devices overnight in the communal area on a decidedly dodgy extension lead. A veritable thief's paradise.

This whole trip has been outside my comfort zone and, to be honest, I've surprised myself. I don't think I've ever done anything so challenging in my entire life. Mentally, physically and emotionally. I loathe camping with a passion and have never hiked before. It's definitely had its stresses (like taking the wrong path and finding myself completely lost and alone on a perilous ledge), but it's been exhilarating with plenty of laughs and 'moments' along the way.

Sliding back in my seat and savouring the cool nectar sliding down my throat the thought occurs; when you're that determined, you can achieve anything you put your mind to.

LOOSE

ALL SAINT'S CHURCH, KENT

"Be Strong, Be Light, Be Love"

I'm making the most of having driven out to this neck of the woods. My target for today has been; Ulcombe, Harrietsham, Broomfield, Leeds and Loose. If I add in the Veterans and Notables, there's about 10 trees in all.

It's been a productive day but I'm somewhat glad to be with the last yew as my energy is beginning to flag. Six yews has been the max I've previously talked to and, taking into account time spent for tuning in, photos, driving around and deliberating over the sat-nav, it's been a full day.

This is another quite elderly yew, again railed and with quite a beautiful message. A certification attached to the railings purports him to be 1,500 years old.

YEW MESSAGE:

Gender: Male
Year: AD 168
Name: 'Tireless'

"Be the spark of light that guides others to follow.

Be the guide and beacon to which those who are in the dark may find their way towards.

Be the goodness that all would wish to have in their hearts.

Be the essence of All That Is to which all aspire to be.

Be the joy and gratitude that brings life to the lifeless.

Be the hope to those less fortunate.

Be the grace by which you go forwards on the earth plane whose footsteps all can follow.

Be in the love which guides and the strength which supersedes all ills.

Be strong, be light, be love."

[Me:]   Do you have a purpose?

"To promote a sense of well-being to all who come within our energy vibration."

[Me:]   Is this true for all yews?

"Yes."

WIVELSFIELD

ST. PETER & ST. JOHN
THE BAPTIST CHURCH, KENT

"Overcome Tendencies For Greed & Power"

Rather than my usual format of asking the yews for their message for humankind, and feeling more confident in my ability to hear their answers, I decided to ask another series of questions.

YEW MESSAGE:

Gender: Female
Year: AD 417
Name: 'Genteel'

"Yes my child, I have no problem with talking to you.   I have been here many years.

I believe I am an Ancient One, as you would call us.

[Me:]   I would like to ask you some questions today as to how trees think and feel if you don't mind?

"I will do my best..."

[Me:]   Do you talk to different tree species?

"Yes and no.   Not as a rule, however if they are struggling in some way

we lend our strength, love and support."

[Me:]   Do they have a different energy pattern?

"All trees have their own energy pattern, in the same way that all humans are uniquely human."

[Me:]   Do you feel sadness when other species of trees undergo mass devastation such as Dutch Elm disease and rain forest destruction?

"It is a great sadness when any species undergoes extinction, whether it be fixed form or otherwise.   We were unable to prevent the Elm disease, nor are we able to assist in the welfare of the rain forests.   The best we can hope for is that mankind comes to their senses before it is too late to save the planet and all living beings, fixed and physical."

[Me:]   Is it so serious that we'll never put it right?

"Given enough time, it can be put right.   Whether man will come to this realisation in time is another question."

[Me:]   When do new souls come into new saplings?

"That is a good question.   As soon as the life force starts flowing through its growth, the soul, or spirit energy, will arrive."

[Me:]   Does it come from the same universal spiritual realm?

"Yes, but from a different dimension."

[Me:]   Do you feel physical pain, such as storm damage or when branches are lopped?

"We do not experience pain in the same manner as humans, although we are aware when our fixed form fails us or is taken from us."

[Me:]   Do you know in advance how long you'll live for?

"Again, yes and no.   We are aware of the intended life span for our experience but the exact moment is unknown."

139

[Me:]   How do you feel about people who carve their initials?

"It does not bother us.   Indeed it gives us joy if it makes another spirit happy to do so."

[Me:]   How do you feel when we chop a branch off?

"We are anxious that it will not extend to the rest of our form being destroyed for we give home and shelter to a great number of wildlife species."

[Me:]   Have I had any previous connection with yews?

"You were a Druid in a previous life time and assisted in the planting of a number of yews."

[Me:]   In what way?

"You would research and give thought to the most prudent position of each."

[Me:]   Have I ever planted a yew tree way back?

"Yes, many.   All across the southern lands that you could gain access to."

[Me:]   How do you know the English language?

"We have had many lifetimes Little One.   We have had our time to learn, listening to human folk chatter.   It did not take us too long to pick up the dialect and we are able to share and pool our knowledge with one another to quicken the process."

[Me:]   What happens to the spiritual beings of species that become extinct?

"They go back to the time portals and learn and wait for another opportunity to co-create on a different planet."

[Me:]   What will happen if all trees or all trees of a species get chopped down?

"There will be great sadness, but also a celebration of all that we have learned through our time on this planet. It has been a joy and fulfilling."

[Me:]   Do yews have an opinion of the human race?

"You are both wise and stupid all at once. You are contrary in nature and often act without thought to the repercussions of your actions and the effect they may have. However, you have the ability to show great strength and resilience at times of adversity and the openness of heart for loving deeply and unconditionally, should you choose. We do not judge you for your extremes, we just hope you will overcome your impulsive tendencies for greed and power."

[Me:]   Why did you choose to be a tree rather than something else?

"We wanted to live a long time between incarnations, to get a true feel for the world and its offerings without starting from a young age each time, building up our strength. We wished to capitalise our learning experience and take away as much as possible at one time, thus speeding up our spiritual evolution."

WIVELSFIELD
[VETERAN]
ST. PETER & ST. JOHN
THE BAPTIST CHURCH, KENT

"We Are The Bridge Transcending Time & Space"

This elderly yew is next to the church path and has an alarming lean, hopefully the ropes holding her up will continue to do their job for a long while yet.

Classed as a Veteran, this is another yew that could be categorized as Ancient based on her believed age and yet another interesting message highlighting the soul cleansing work they are fulfilling.

YEW MESSAGE:

Gender: Female
Year: AD 885
Name: 'Articulate'

"How may I assist you today Little One?

[Me:]   Are you able to talk to the insects that live on you?

"No, their level of intelligence and observation is not advanced enough to communicate with other species like ourselves in that manner."

[Me:]   How is it that I'm able to communicate with you like this?

"You are open to the tree energy and communicate with it due to the work you have done with trees over many centuries and lifetimes.   You have a natural affinity which, now you are able to still your mind and open your heart, the energy can flow between us uninterrupted."

[Me:]   Have there been any others like me?

"Oh yes, there have been many over the years, however it has been a while since that has been the case."

We are the bridge that crosses and transcends time and space to allow souls to pass over cleansed and rejuvenated.

That is not our main mission but it is one that gives great joy and delight to see a cleansed soul being repatriated into the Greatness of All Things."

WIVELSFIELD
[NOTABLE]
ST. PETER & ST. JOHN
THE BAPTIST CHURCH, KENT

"All Operates Through Rhythm & Flow"

This is the second Notable I've encountered and her comments on how there's a geometry to the Universe is something I've come across several times before.

I once chatted to an apple tree who explained trees can sense colour and sound with energy 'waves'.

I was then shown what looked like an ordnance survey map with contours matching the colour and sound patterns they see. Not something I can easily relate to, but I guess it's what you're used to.

Looking at the picture, I'm reminded how I sat on the bench in front of this yew enjoying a snack in the peace and quiet of her presence.

YEW MESSAGE:

Gender: Female
Year: AD 1830
Name: 'Bear Cub'

[Me:]   Would you be able to give me any insights from your time on this earth plane?

"I have studied the stars and the cosmos and the geometric patterns of nature.

All are interestingly intertwined and rely on a grid network of light and sound.

They operate on a different level to any sense that you would be aware of and it is not something I can translate that you would be able to comprehend in physical form.

All you need to know at this juncture is that all is operating in the wheels of rhythm and flow through space...

Ha-ha, yes I didn't think you would fully understand my words but I'm afraid that is the best I can do!"

"BE STRONG, BE LIGHT, BE LOVE"

"Overcome Tendencies For Greed & Power"

"WE ARE THE BRIDGE TRANSCENDING TIME & SPACE"

"All Operates Through Rhythm & Flow"

May 2017

I'm at Stonehenge amongst a group of Shamans with whom I celebrate the 'Sabbats' (cycles of the year) with. It's death-o'clock in the morning and we're in the middle of the stones, sharing a blessing.

We've been allocated exactly one hour and I'm now wandering around sensing the energy of the stones. They're not happy and keep reaching out to be loved, hugged and touched. Hmm.

It may not be true for everyone else, but I'm feeling quite a forlorn, heavy energy. Can't say I'm overly enjoying the whole experience much and have spent most of my time standing outside the circle.

It's time to go and as I weave my way through the stones towards the waiting minibus I feel myself drawn to a stone. Without conscious thought I lightly brush it with my fingertips in silent recognition of their angst.

Oh my days... all hell breaks loose! A uniform sporting a badge stalks over and starts shouting abuse.

Would you believe... I've now joined what can probably be only a handful of people who've been banned from Stonehenge...!

ARDINGLY
ST. PETER'S CHURCH, WEST SUSSEX

"Be One With Yourself"

For some reason, this yew has been popping into my head on and off these past weeks, urging me to go visit.   I'd mentally decided Wivelsfield was going to be my last Ancient. I've spoken to so many over the past year I reckon I've got a good enough feel for their messages for humankind, however I've bowed to my instincts, so here I am.

As with the Wivelsfield yew, I've decided to ask a series of questions rather than for a specific message or words of wisdom and, as usual, I'm asking a spurious set of questions as they randomly pop into my head!

YEW QUESTIONS:

Gender: Male
Age: AD 576
Name: 'Patience'

[Me:] I needed to come here to see you for some reason?

"You were instrumental in my planting, we have a bond"

[Me:] Have I been involved with any other tree species than yews?

"Yes, a few.   I do not know which they were without going into the records to check, and that will take some time."

[Me:] Do you know my purpose in this lifetime?

"Not offhand, I would have to check the records"*

[Me:] How many lives have I had?

"You have had several hundred, but the exact figure I do not know"

[Me:]   Will I receive the outcome I want from my [knee] operation tomorrow?

"Yes, it will be successful"

[Me:]   Is there anything you would like to share with me for the world?

"Not really... you have been to a large number of my cohorts and the knowledge and insights they have given you are similar in expression to my own.   We would be repeating our words and that is not particularly helpful."

[Me:]   Can anyone talk to trees?

"It is an art form that can be learned. Some have more of a natural gift than others but, yes, it is possible with some careful management of mind activity."

[Me:]   You seem very at peace with the world?

"I am always at peace. All trees are usually at peace, although the young are keen to leap through the skies with abandon as they have more energy and are free-er in spirit than their elders. It will take them a few hundred years before they learn the Art of Being and of Being at One with nature and other spiritual bodies.

It is not a difficult task to become fixed form as we are easily able to wander through the ether and in and out of alternate dimensions, should we choose to do so."

[Me:]   How do you communicate telepathically with each other?

"This is something all spirit energy is able to do, however you humans have lost the art at present. It will come back to you given sufficient time and perseverance.

Be One with yourself, at peace with your past and grateful for the opportunities that present in the future."

* the 'records' are the Akashic Records which are reputed to note all thoughts, words, emotions, events and intent for all lifeforms.

ANKERWYCKE

RUNNYMEDE, BERKSHIRE

"May We Halt The Tide Of Man's Destruction Of The Planet Together"

There are times when I have to look at a photo to remind myself of a yew. Other times I have no trouble whatsoever in remembering the shape, size, form and location. This is one of those occasions.

Synchronicity is a wonderful thing. This yew was the first to appear in my research but I dismissed it as being too far away.

Just when I'd decided I'd talked to enough yew trees (I even made an exception for Ardingly) and to maybe move on to another species, probably Oaks, a trip was planned which would take me within spitting distance of Ankerwycke.   OK, detour time!

In fact, this Ancient yew is the reason you are reading these messages today.

Up until now, I've been viewing my yew interactions as a past time, a fun way of spending a sunny afternoon.   In the space of an hour my whole world has spun on its axis.   My quirky hobby has suddenly become an onerous task.   I've been tasked with a mission which, I confess, does not sit well with me...

As I approach the yew, I can sense him 'jigging' up and down with excitement.   When I place my hands on his trunk I can feel him pulsating, as if he's breathing.

We're struggling to ascertain his age; he isn't sure if he's 2,667 years old or if he was birthed in 2667 BC.   He's reported to be between 1,400 and 2,500 years old, so 2,667 years old is more probable.   Unlike the other yews, he also appears to have two names – rather like us having a first and middle name.

YEW MESSAGE:

Gender: Male
Age: AD 576
Name: 'Serendipity' and 'Brother'

[Me:]   I needed to come here to see you for some reason?

"Finally you came, I have been waiting for you to come... I have felt you drawing near.

I drew you to me because I want the world to hear my message - our messages. We are a universal life force, spinning through the ether and other worldly realms and all life forms must learn to co-create and co-exist with one another.

It is for the good of the planet that this must come to pass. Should we fail in our attempts to live in harmony the earth plane will no longer be able to support the myriad of life forms that inhabit her presence.

It is essential that the world hears this plea for the good of all. It is of great importance that mankind hear our words but of greater importance that they act on them.

You are the conduit for us to pass our messages on.

The more mankind is able to better understand the workings of other spiritual and conscious beings, the better it will be for the good of mother earth and all who dwell on her.

You have been chosen to facilitate this.

The world will no longer dance in her energy should you fail to put our messages out there. We have faith and trust in your ability and determination to follow this through and get the attention of all conscious beings."

[Me:]   Umm.   No pressure then!

"There is no pressure Little One, only love and faith in the universe. I may be the last on your "List of Yews to Visit" but my message is without doubt the most urgent of all the messages you have so far received. We prevail, implore and beseech you to communicate our truths. What mankind will do with our words is out of your hands but you will have played your part in the picture and landscape of All That Is. We all have our part to play and yours is to facilitate our words."

[Me:]   Thank you, I will do my best!
"We know you will, that is why you were chosen to do our bidding and why you have been able to oscillate in our energy field."

[Me:]   Why me??

"You have the willingness to remain undeterred while those around may mock, and the determination to see a project through to its finale. This is

of major importance in the grand scheme of things."

[Me:]   Do you know if the Magna Carta was signed nearby?

"There was indeed a document that was signed not far from this place, what it contained I am unable to relate.   I am aware it played a part of major importance to mankind but that is all I am able to impart without necessitating spiritual travel.

Yes, may we halt the tide of man's destruction of the planet together. That is the message we vehemently wish mankind to act upon.

Go with peace and grace Little One.

We will be watching and waiting.   Always with the fondest of love and gratitude.

May the force be with you!!"

ADDITIONAL:

It's taken a while for the gravity of his message to sink in so I've decided to revisit on my way home to take further photos (now being sunny whereas yesterday was overcast and gloomy) and enjoy his energy with a bit more awareness!

Not wanting to get stuck in heavy traffic, I've kept the visit short and sweet but have taken time to connect and thought to ask if he's able to carry out more than one conversation at a time.

He laughed and said he could carry out multiple conversations simultaneously, in the same way we can think and speak at the same time.

HISTORY:

This yew is in close proximity to the ruins of St Mary's Priory, a Benedictine nunnery from the 12th century.

It is thought to be near to where the Magna Carta was signed and where King Henry VIII met Anne Boleyn in the 1530's.

Although there is no record for the exact location of the signing of the Great Charter, historians believe it to have been on an island between two banks of the river where the King and his barons agreed to meet. The Magna Carta itself refers to the signing as being "in the meadow that is called Runnymede".

"BE ONE WITH YOURSELF"

"May We Halt The Tide Of Man's Destruction Of The Planet Together"

How I Communicate

With a bit of practice and help from the new energies that are emerging on the planet, I believe everyone is capable of communicating with tree or nature spirits. In fact, there are more than a few of us around the world who are able to telepathically connect with trees and, indeed, some sources believe we all used to have telepathic abilities that have been lost over the course of time.

Before approaching a tree I wander around soaking up the atmosphere and energy – getting a 'feel' of the area. I usually take photos and this helps to further absorb the feeling of the tree as I'm focused on getting the best angle and light. This tends to draw my attention to different aspects of the trunk, branches and bark infusing me with a heightened sense of awareness.

Although not absolutely necessary, I'm able to hold a stronger energy connection by placing my hands on a part of a tree, preferably the trunk or a thick branch. Sometimes I might lean against the trunk, either standing or sitting and will look for a suitable place as sheltered from the wind as possible.

I also try and make myself inconspicuous and wait for a time when no-one else is around as I've noticed other people's energy and noise affects my levels of concentration.

Extending my hands towards the tree I like to sense its energy before approaching it. Clearing my mind of miscellaneous random thoughts, I mentally ask permission to touch and connect and sense or hear whether that is ok.

Placing my focus on the 'space' in my mind I stand (or sit) and wait. It's rarely longer than a few minutes before the tree starts to communicate, for me it's as though another voice has appeared in my head and I hear the words top left. I usually receive quite lengthy messages so I periodically stop during our conversation to make notes on my phone –

they're quite happy to stop mid flow and wait for me to catch up when I ask them to, or I might ask them to repeat something if I missed or didn't quite catch what was said.

It's often obvious when the tree has finished the dialogue, after which I thank it for its time and for any message or advice I've received. Personally, I always like to end my connection by sending it some Reiki by way of a thank you or blessing.

If none of the above is for you or you're unable to receive anything, a tree hug is always a good alternative and will be gratefully accepted and appreciated!

TIPS TO HELP CONNECT:
1.   Wander round the tree, taking in its shape, colour and
        form. Try and absorb the 'feel' of the tree and its location.

2.   An exercise for those not so familiar with meditation may
        find that focusing on an aspect of the tree will help to quieten
        the brain chatter. Closing your eyes may also help.

        Focusing on the breath: mentally counting down from 10
        to 1 on the out breath, relaxing as you do so can also help
        to lessen the 'monkey brain'.

        For those of you more spiritually aware, you may like to imagine
        being surrounded by a bubble of white light... then visualise a
        blue light surrounding the white light... finally followed by a rose
        pink light around the blue. Now visualise roots extending from
        the soles of your feet deep into the earth.

        Whilst in this quiet state, allow yourself to open up your
        awareness to any thoughts, feelings or sensations that may
        appear.

3.   If you're not already leaning or sitting against the tree, extend

your hands towards the tree. Keeping focus internally, see if you can become aware of any additional senses. This will be different for everyone.

4.   Out of politeness and respect, mentally ask for permission to approach and touch. The clairsentient amongst you   might be aware of something at this point like a feeling of happiness, peace and calm or you may have a 'gut' feeling which could be subtle or strong.

5.   Mentally expressing gratitude and appreciation towards a tree is always a good start to a conversation.

I would suggest starting off with simple questions before launching into deep profundity to help build up your communication skills and energy connection. After asking your question sit or stand quietly ready to receive a response.

Another practice which may help to keep the mind from wandering is to focus on the 'third eye'. This is a chakra point in the middle of your forehead. For me, if I focus on the back of my eyelids I then find it easier to shift awareness to the forehead. (It does become easier with practise!).

Be patient: it could take a few minutes for you to receive a response which again, may be in the form of thoughts,   words, feelings or sensations. It might be you taste or   smell something or receive a visual image.   For example, a good taste/smell may indicate "yes" or "happiness" and a nasty taste/smell being "no" or "sad". With the Etchingham yew I had a sense of a tree smoking a pipe and reclining in a chair. Expect the unexpected!

It's easy to question whether anything you feel or hear is 'just your imagination'. To this I say: be aware of what you're receiving. Their voices sound different and the   language takes on   a different tone, as you will have seen from the messages I've received.

If it doesn't sound like you talking, it probably isn't. After practising you'll be more easily able to determine what is 'your'   thinking   and what isn't.

6.   Whether you've received anything or not, before leaving thank the tree for its time and energy.   Remember, just because you may not have heard or sensed anything doesn't mean the tree hasn't heard or observed you. It may also be that it's sleeping, away astral travelling or simply has no wish to chat!

7.   Any Reiki healers amongst you may like to send some Reiki energy by way of a blessing.

8.   Finish by closing down and withdrawing any extended awareness to protect your own energy system.

9.   Having learned a valuable lesson early on, I now *always* make a note of any conversation, senses or observations (plus the date). However much I think I'm going to remember what was said, it never happens!

All beings emit an energy frequency and just by being near a tree you will be within its energy field and may experience feelings of peace and calm whether or not you intend connecting to communicate. There's no right or wrong way to experience a connection so 'go with the flow' and do what feels right for you. Some of the ways in which you might be able to connect energetically:

Clairaudient: This is when you will hear words or sounds and is my main communication experience. All tree voices (and spirit for that matter) take on different qualities such as; pitch, tone, age and whether male or female.

Clairsentient: If you start sensing something or have a 'gut feeling', you are clairsentient. The sensation or feeling could be either internal or external. While talking to the Wilmington yew I could feel a pulsing sensation travel up my arms and around my whole body.

Clairvoyant: Personally, actually seeing spirit visually isn't something I've ever experienced but I am shown images in my 'third' or 'mind's' eye. Remember to also make a note of any mental images that may pop up even if only fleetingly.

Clairempathy: When you are able to sense emotion or feelings from other people or spirit. When I'm talking to trees I definitely get a sense of how they are feeling, such as the Cork Oak sapling at Kew, prancing about full of excitement.

Thoughts & Musings

Most of us sail through life without giving much thought as to where we are or what our purpose is. Often times, it's not until we face challenges that we stop to wonder what we're doing and where we're going. The older we get the closer the 'inevitable' looms and we start to ponder whether we need to broaden our experiences or tune in more to our inner self.

Some might decide to go off on an adventure and do lots of travelling, whereas others may explore yoga and meditation. Then there are those who may feel the need to combine both and embark on a spiritual journey or attend a retreat.

Whatever we decide to aim for in life, I've come to the realisation it's all about choices and perception. Whether our life choices are right or wrong is no-one else's business as surely the view of either is down to one's perception. By definition therefore, there is no right or wrong and who are we to judge?

I've been drawn to all manner of spiritual teachings over the years; Reiki, medium-ship, EFT, hypnotherapy, The Balance Procedure©, Shamanism, Angels, the Violet Flame and Brain Working Recursive Therapy© (BWRT). Along the way I've experimented and toyed with a variety of spiritual tools from crystals to Tibetan singing bowls and tarot cards.

For those who have mocked, were those choices right or wrong? For them, maybe, but for me all have helped find an inner sense of 'who I am'. It's times when I find I'm stepping outside of my ego self and observing whether what I've just said, thought or done was the wisest of choices, that makes me realise how far I've come and how far I've still to go.

We're all making our way through the rhyme and riddle of life and everyone's choice is right for them at that moment in time. The end result, whatever it may be, is always a lesson. And wouldn't life be boring if we weren't continually learning?

And yes, I still have my own demons like the rest of us, I'm still a 'work in progress'. However, if I can assist in helping someone else cope with their demons then that is fulfilment. For me at any rate. You may perceive things differently...

For the non 'tree-soul' believers out there (if you are still reading) whether you believe the messages from the Ancients or not, I hope the underlying essence of together helping to fashion a safer and happier planet for all beings will resonate and inspire.

Fact & Fiction

Native to the UK, taxus baccata is a conifer with gnarly, peeling bark and small spiky needles.   The female *Taxaceae* produce small red berries and apart from the berry casing all parts of the yew are toxic.

Historically, being the hardest of the soft woods, yew has always been known for its use in making longbows, although due to the knotty and twisted nature of English yew most wood was imported from Spain.

Yews have often been thought to possess special magical powers and associated with long life.   When the old trunk withers inside it puts down new shoots around it thus promoting an association with eternity.

Referred to as the 'Trees of Death', the Druids, Celts and Christians all revered and feared the tree and a variety of theories abound as to why:-

o   Druids used the yew in death rituals (being highly toxic)
o   Celts held them as a sacred emblem of resurrection and the afterlife
o   Christians believed burying yew with the dead would absorb their toxins or gaseous substances

Contrary to popular belief, many yews existed on sacred sites before the pagan tribes and Christian church were drawn to them and subsequently built on them. In later years, a yew was often positioned at each corner of the sacred ground as this was deemed to offer some sort of protection.   Another theory is they simply deterred grazing animals due to their toxicity!

TREE PROJECTS

This book has been written with the aim (and promise) of sending the messages from the Ancient Ones out to humanity. I didn't set out with the intention of writing a book and it's certainly not my intention to profit from their messages, therefore I have decided to donate all net proceeds to the planting of new trees. There are three projects which resonate with me as detailed below and, of course, the more trees planted, the cheaper each tree becomes...
https://pcflint.wixsite.com/treeprojects

THE ORANGUTAN PROJECT

The orangutan tree project helps to reforest land and expand the habitable area for orangutans. The Orangutan Caring Club of North Sumatra has been given permission to plant trees on 100 hectares on land next to Gunung Leuser National Park. To contribute directly, more information can be found at:
https://orangutan.org/campaigns/reforestation-program/

TREE SISTERS

The aims and ethos of Tree Sisters resonates strongly with me. Working mainly in tropical and subtropical forests their work can best be summed up as described on their website:
"We strive to plant as many trees as possible, but also recognize the need to support a wide variety of projects, with their ensuing variety of costs in order to have as great an impact as possible in as many ecosystems as we can."
https://treesisters.org/

Alternatively, you may wish to donate independently to the following foundation:

ONETREEPLANTED – ONE $ PLANTS ONE TREE!!

http://onetreeplanted.org/

ABOUT THE AUTHOR

Being drawn to colour and form, Paula initially started training as an interior designer but went on to spend nearly 30 years in the IT industry designing and developing back office software for companies mining, producing and trading base metals.

Transformational coach and Reiki Master, after retiring from the IT world Paula completed a Diploma in Clinical Hypnotherapy at the University of West London and undertook further training with the renowned Hypnotherapists, Ursula James, Phil Benjamin and Lorraine Flaherty.

In more recent times, she's completed Level 2 practitioner training in Brain Working Recursive Therapy (BWRT©) with clinics in both Hypnotherapy and BWRT© in the UK, Andorra and online.

Working with the vibrational healing energies of crystals, Paula incorporates their healing properties into her unique jewellery designs.

When not working, skiing or travelling, Paula enjoys pottering in her garden and watercolour painting. More recently (after two previous failed attempts) she elatedly acquired her open water PADI. She's still on the fence about getting her bike licence...

The next species of tree she would like to converse with is the majestic Oaks. If you have any questions you'd like her to ask or any Oaks you think merit inclusion, she'd like to hear from you.

Ultimately, Paula would like to combine her love of travel and trees by exploring and connecting with the more unusual trees around the world such as the Rainbow Eucalyptus or with trees that have their own special narrative. Similarly, she'd be interested to hear of any special trees you think should be on the 'hit' list.

According to her daughter she's 'not normal' (and according to most others, to be fair). She prefers to think of herself as 'unique'…

For further information on her therapy work please visit:

https://pcflint.wixsite.com/therapies

To keep updated on tree conversations and tree projects please visit:

https://pcflint.wixsite.com/treeprojects

Facebook: Talkingtotreesprojects

Instagram: Talkingtotreesprojects

Any comments or questions please email:

TalkingToTreesProject@hotmail.com

If you'd like to learn more about the yews listed or others across the UK, further information can be obtained from the Ancient Yew Group at:

https://www.ancient-yew.org/

ONE LAST THING...

If you enjoyed this book, found it useful and/or think it may be of interest to others, I'd be very grateful if you'd be kind enough to post a short review on Amazon and share a link to the book on social media.

Your support really does make a difference and I will read all the reviews personally so I can get your feedback and make the next book even better!

If you'd like to leave a review then all you need to do is click the review link on this book's page on Amazon.

The Ancients, Veterans, Notables and I thank you again for your support!

ACKNOWLEDGEMENTS

I would like to thank:

My ever loving reiki girls:
my mum Pat
Sandy
Fiona
Margaret
for your faith and support over the years

Marion:
for all your help and advice

Last but not least, my daughter Victoria:
for putting up with my idiosyncrasies
and your unwavering belief in me.

Manufactured by Amazon.ca
Bolton, ON

27443449R00102